THE
SECULAR
EXPERIENCE
OF
GOD

Christian Mission and Modern Culture

EDITED BY
ALAN NEELY, H. WAYNE PIPKIN,
AND WILBERT R. SHENK

In the Series:

THE
SECULAR
EXPERIENCE
OF
GOD

KENNETH CRAGG

TRINITY PRESS
INTERNATIONAL
HARRISBURG, PENNSYLVANIA

First published by
TRINITY PRESS INTERNATIONAL
P.O. Box 1321
Harrisburg, PA 17105
U.S.A.

First British edition
published by
GRACEWING
2 Southern Avenue
Leominster
Herefordshire HR6 0QF
England

Trinity Press International is a division of the Morehouse Group.

Cover design: Brian Preuss

Library of Congress Cataloging-in-Publication Data

Cragg, Kenneth.
    The secular experience of God / Kenneth Cragg.
        p.   cm. — (Christian mission and modern culture)
    Includes bibliographical references
    ISBN 1-56338-223-7 (alk. paper)
    1. Secularization (Theology)   2. Missions—Theory.   I. Title.
II. Series.
BT83.7.C78   1998
261—dc21   97-41102
                                                                CIP

Gracewing ISBN: 0-85244-482-6

Printed in the United States of America

98 99 00 01 02 6 5 4 3 2 1

Contents

Preface to the Series

Both Christian mission and modern culture, widely regarded as antagonists, are in crisis. The emergence of the modern mission movement in the early nineteenth century cannot be understood apart from the rise of technocratic society. Now, at the end of the twentieth century, both modern culture and Christian mission face an uncertain future.

One of the developments integral to modernity was the way the role of religion in culture was redefined. Whereas religion had played an authoritative role in the culture of Christendom, modern culture was highly critical of religion and increasingly secular in its assumptions. A sustained effort was made to banish religion to the backwaters of modern culture.

The decade of the 1980s witnessed further momentous developments on the geopolitical front with the collapse of communism. In the aftermath of the breakup of the system of power blocs that dominated international relations for a generation, it is clear that religion has survived even if its institutionalization has undergone deep change and its future forms are unclear. Secularism continues to oppose religion, while technology has emerged as a major source of power and authority in modern culture. Both confront Christian faith with fundamental questions.

The purpose of this series is to probe these developments from a variety of angles with a view to helping the church understand its missional responsibility to a culture in crisis. One important resource is the church's experience of two centuries of cross-cultural mission that has reshaped the church into a global Christian *ecumene.* The focus of our inquiry will be the church in modern culture. The series (1) examines modern/postmodern culture from a missional point of view; (2) develops the theological agenda that the church in modern culture must address in order to recover its own integrity; and (3) tests fresh conceptualizations of the nature and mission of the church as it engages modern culture. In other words, these volumes are intended to be a forum where conventional assumptions can be challenged and alternative formulations explored.

This series is a project authorized by the Institute of Mennonite Studies, research agency of the Associated Mennonite Biblical Seminary, and supported by a generous grant from the Pew Charitable Trusts.

Editorial Committee

ALAN NEELY
H. WAYNE PIPKIN
WILBERT R. SHENK

1

Exploring an Irony

"The Secular Experience of God"? The title seems incongruous. Is not "experience" cumulative, hazardous, at best progressive, at worst ambiguous and desolating? How can experience, a very mortal commodity, apply to the Eternal? The adjective "secular," too, is impossible. What is divine, we must suppose, is thereby sacred.

"Experience" (*experientia*), however, also means "being put to the test"; and ever since Job, the man from the land of Uz, this has been happening to God. It has been the stock-in-trade of theology as an intellectual ambition toward the love of God. It has been even more frequent in the haunts of suffering and oppression. In the corridors of power, too, the divine has been subjected to endless invocations, annexations, and controversies. Will it then be invalid in these pages to explore contemporary secularization as, at least conceptually, "happening to God"? Demise, abolition, death, burial—ever since Nietzsche these are said to have occurred in heaven.

Further, as grammarians remind us, genitives are both objective and subjective. It will make sense to study the experience of God that secular people undergo, if only in what the eclipse, the elision, the redundancy, of the divine dimension means. What happens in the heart when the place earlier occupied by God is discovered to be vacant certainly amounts to a significant secular experience. Whether it be liberation, desolation, loss, gain, confusion, panic, or inquietude, it is certain that secularity is not indifferently rid of God. Denial, or abrogation, is meaningless about nonentities.

Depending on what we can let ourselves believe, the subjective genitive may also have its point. What might all these attitudes, reactions, and decisions in the human sphere imply for the eternal party to them? The course of thought needs to be careful here. The philosophic idea of God is of inviolable otherness, sublimity immune from all that conditions human awareness. Serene, even oblivious or—otherwise—implacable, the God of Plato, Aristotle, and Spinoza admits no human cares. "Secular" or any other "experience" could never be postulated of any deity intelligibly or properly divine.

With Yahweh in the Hebrew Scriptures, however, this is not so. Yahweh is believed to be capable of every kind of passion, yearning, grief, zeal, and blazing anger. "The Lord thy God is a jealous God," suitably served by the ardor of his Elijahs avenging his rivals, his inferiors, the upstart Baalim, the fertility lords of pagan illusion. The Yahweh of Hosea pleads and mourns with urgent human wistfulness and pain: "O Israel, how shall I give thee up?" The prophet's bitter domestic tragedy of betrayal is the very matrix of his perception of divine tenderness and of the deep woundedness of Yahweh.

These biblical perceptions leave us with deep problems. How to reconcile them with the legitimate meaning of divine impassibility has long been a central preoccupation of theology. A sense of total irreconcilability here has been among the powerful stimuli of secular agnosticism. It must have due place in later pages. For the present, however, if divine imperviousness to the tragedy of the human predicament has been for many the decisive logic in skepticism, it is plainly a logic saying that perviousness *ought* to be the divine quality. Believers and skeptics alike are agreed on the necessity. In this sense their criteria for God converge, and the question between them is not whether *conceptually*, but whether *actually*.

Perhaps nowhere was the point more neatly caught than in Paul's discourse on the Areopagus among the Athenian literati about the inscription on the wayside shrine. The words *Agnosto Theo* (Acts 17:23) were an agnostic tribute to an agnostic deity. "To the god whom it may concern" is the sense. Deities could indeed be indifferent yet be in high dudgeon about not being regarded by humans. Hence there is the precaution of placating, by a legend on stone, a deity who may exist unknown to us, or whose name we cannot identify, or who presides over this stretch of the road. (Waymarks at that time were religious, identifying the hovering patrons of the territory.) Obviously negligent about their duties, for they had omitted the basic one of disclosing themselves, such gods were in no way negligent about their due recognition; so discreet, wary, and precarious mortals worshiped in ignorance of whom they worshiped. Unpredictability was their major assumption about deities. The final question was and is the quality of the relevance. This issue goes to the heart of secularity.

In the pagan world of Greek and Roman antiquity, atheism was not an option. Nor, equally, was faith. All was credulity; there were no credible credentials offered or required. Paganism consisted of rites and rituals to be performed. These were simply to be done. They had no status as the conviction of intelligent search. When Roman emperors demanded worship, the rationale was entirely political, not intellectual. Faith as authentic, decisive confidence in divine credentials came with Christianity—faith historically grounded, accessible to mind, and humanly inclusive without duress and without ethnic limits.[1] "Whom it *does* concern" was Christian language, understanding itself as warranted by proof of divine relevance in the Christ-event. It was not persuaded of God by dint of a private providence like the Exodus. That precedent served it well, but only by lending its imagery to the comprehension of a climax in Messiah-Jesus incorporating all humankind in an inclusive redemption.

It will be evident later how vital this perspective is to any intelligent theism responding to secularity. For, in its most characteristic idiom, secularity amounts to an attitude that assumes the negligibility of God to the point where it is no longer necessary to deny him. Unlike atheism, which is concerned to deny, disprove, and denounce, secularity finds this scarcely required. We are simply on our own (cf. Murdoch 1970:79).

Discussion as to the existence of God was always somewhat fatuous, *relevance* being the real question. The irrelevance so readily concluded in the contemporary West spells nonexistence so effectively that a rationally based case for atheism needs no making. The irony is profound. We seem to have arrived at a point where the transcendent is entirely contingent—a contingency turning on human whims that are becoming increasingly whimsical. Do we have to conclude that the being of God has always turned on human religiousness, a commodity that is now in ever shorter supply? If so, no more altars are necessary, for they could only be inscribed: "*From* whom it is of no concern."

Against such a plausible conclusion, however, two contentions assert themselves. Transcendence has at all costs to be reaffirmed, first as an institutional necessity, and second, as a spiritual vocation. The one is a rigorous championing of God's interests in sharply custodial ways that repudiate all ideas of God's negligence, thereby reinstating the divine in inexorable terms. The other reads indifference to, or nonexperience of, God as a summons to more patient interpretation of ethical reality. It accepts that the bewilderment about divine relevance, rather than the bare category of existence, is deeply present and deserves an honest reckoning. It is ready to undertake secularity on secularity's own terms as, in effect, a plea for more authentic religion. It will perceive a genuine "secular experience of God" in the very situation that challenges theology.

Each of these two responses to the seeming negligibility of God and contemporary secularity suggests ironies going further still. To note them may set a sort of agenda for all the tasks ahead in these pages. One irony is that the champions of divine claims, institutionalized in structures of belief, ritual, and code, may well involve secular folk in an experience of God likely to be characterized by tyranny, obscurantism, spiritual distress, or mental pain. These, aimed at reversing the negligibility of God, may well deepen the will for it. In aiming to regiment society back into something theocratic, whether in personal status law (as in Israel) or under closed interpretations of Islamic Shari'ah, they may have their way, partially or fully, but only at the expense of the most deeply religious things—namely, liberty, honesty, and compassion. Such are the fundamentalisms.

Many efforts after an imposed structure of divine relevance will have some affinity with the old Roman notion of a deified emperor, the logic of which was akin to the *cuius regio eius religio* principle of historic Christendom and the early modern European nation-state. The worship of the emperor symbolized the supremacy of Rome, the sanctity of the state. Power required that quasi-religious sanction. To refuse it was, on the part of the early church, an act of treason, defiant but also obstinate, for "worship" meant no more than political prudence.[2] In its Christendom form, the expectation was that believer and citizen could, should, and must be identical. To belong meant to believe. Society needed the cohesion of a single faith, uniting the population under a single heaven.

Insofar as secularity means and intends a sort of privatization of beliefs and worship, so that these are no legal business of the state, what, we have to ask, becomes of the cohesion of society, the norms, values, and traditions by which alone bodies politic and social identify and know themselves?

Deferring aspects of private religion, the question lands us squarely in the lap of the second response to secular negligence of the transcendent. This can find neither comfort nor wisdom in the "enforcers," but it fears for the san-

ity and security of the social order if and when the transcendent reference is totally forfeited.

ii

It is obvious that what the rigorists hold to be infallibly
indispensable, practice outside can readily handle as fal-
libly superfluous. Yet reflection on this evident phenomenon affords little thoughtful satisfaction and much
unease. The imperatives of dogma and the instincts for
theocracy may be reprehensible, historically guilty, and
spiritually dubious; but the very minds that find them so
are not thereby less wistful for what doctrine should
maintain and sanctify. Negligence of God may be entirely practicable, for a while at least; but an anxiety lurks
around it, a lack registers its sinister implication. We
will note in another context the strange surviving power
of discarded faith. Neglect of mystery and the demise of
wonder take their revenge on the self that sanctions flip-
pancy or forfeits reverence.

There is a nemesis that demands to be heeded. A
verse in the Qur'an captures the point in asking: "Does
man think that he has been left on the loose?" (Surah
75.36). The imagery appears to be that of the tether that
will tug at the soul straying too far.[3] But what, we must
ask, are these constraints that should duly control the
human self and communal society? Was there perhaps,
after all, something appropriate in the age long concepts
of cohesion around dogma, of peoplehood ensured in
rite and symbol with sacrosanct warrant?

Secular alertness to these questions, deterred or
appalled by traditional sacrilizing, and unwilling to
ignore them, may propose a self-reliant solution. Let the
corporate will undertake its own value system, supply

from within its own sanctions, and contrive psychic well-being and social peace by its own energies. Enthrone the "sovereignty of the good," and be self-subjected to a subjective self. The kingdom of God is so far "within you" (Luke 17:21) that it need remain no longer God's but become yours.[4] No adequate realization of the aberrations of organized religion can be insensitive to this stance, for its logic in part arises from the way these have behaved— wherein, again, lies irony. Yet what urgently emerges is whether the transcendent can truly be this way. There are many legitimate reaches of self-discipline, of living by an obedience we have ourselves devised. Yet these are surely contingent on a more inclusive order whose constraints upon us are necessarily absolute and, therefore, not within the contingency of all things human.

But if we are minded to say that such self-generating values are not "letting God be God," is it not clear that the old religious systems were themselves doing that all the time in the different idiom of unworthy dogma or "bad faith"? To have all our values theologically received means an adequately divine perception of the human predicament. In what terms is divine relevance construed both in any faith holding it and in what that faith holds concerning it?

The eminent critic William Hazlitt, commenting on *King Lear* as "the best of all Shakespeare's plays," considered it "the one in which he was the most in earnest" (1906:119). Perhaps that is also the theologically proper criterion. Where is the divine "most in earnest" about us in the human scene or—differently phrased—where or how is divine relevance satisfactorily discerned? Will it be in particular "covenant" and "election" if these are

not eventually and necessarily opened out categorically
to all? Will it be only in law and direction, without cognizance of how these, in their eminently desirable pro-
vision are nevertheless ignored, travestied, and refused?
Will it be in requiring a caste-shaped surrender to a
karmic law so that a fatedness attaches to all our experience? Will it be in a perception of selfhood that reads
time as only a transience and our ego centricity an illusion to forgo?

The supreme irony might thus be that secularity in
its wistful shape is simply searching the religions seriously, requiring their verdicts on the relevance of God.
Finding them inconclusive, unsatisfactory, or obsolete,
it decides to take the missing earnestness upon itself.
Theology, plainly, has more reach than theologians
grasp. To that extent secularity may be their ally, given
a listening ear. All of which leads us into further irony.

iii

The major faiths of the world clearly differ widely in
their capacities for, and resources concerning, current
secularity. Yet the entire situation is a large dimension
of their mutual relations. The cultural equations in
which the issues confront them differ sharply, as do
their calendars of exposure to the demands they make
on the minds of leadership and the instincts of the mass-
es. Judaism and Christianity might be said to be squarely within the modern incidence of the technology that
has so massively contributed to secular perceptions of
divine irrelevance. Islam had its part in the middle centuries in the antecedents of science in the West and
readily accommodates to scientific norms. But the nine-
teenth- and twentieth-century incidence of technology

in Muslim territories has been implicated in circum-
stances of sharp political resentment and ill will. These
have complicated Islamic accommodation to secular factors, tending to a love-hate relation with their sources and
to an often facile acceptance of the means and techniques
along with refusal of the mentality that yielded them.

Asian faiths have been inexorably involved in the
absorption of scientific means and in the political issues
for economies, societies, and cultures that these
entailed. They have thus been radically challenged in
their characteristic evasion of the activism that history
now more than ever requires from faith-adherence. The
emerging colossae of technological capacity in eastern
Asia, in Japan, China, Indonesia, Taiwan, Thailand,
Malaysia, and the Koreas, have entered a single
humanum of technological change, vexing and taxing
their traditional systems and perspectives of what, why,
and whither that *humanum* is.

The question plainly presses concerning how or
whether the major faiths can have any mutual significance in their liabilities to their respective societies.
Secularity interrogates them all. It is a vast commonizer,
searching and shattering their privacies and presenting
them all, alike and differently, with duties to their populations, their demographic factors, their political forms,
and their economic obligations. Their interrelations
have become a crucial element in their inner meaning.
At no time has the world they presume to interpret been
at once so urgently singular and so critically plural.

iv

In reviewing the several ironies present in the secular/
religious situation, we have sketched the themes of a

larger discussion, taking the elements more analytically. It is first important to distinguish, at some length, between secularity in political and legal terms as "neutrality concerning religious belief and allegiance within a given nation or state," and secularity as "a complete repudiation of transcendent reference in private and public realms alike." The terms *secularity* and *secularization* are often used interchangeably. The sense in which either is meant needs to be in careful view. For the "secular state" concept need, in practice, be in no way inimical to personal religious belief nor to its proximate engagement in society and its norms. These issues belong in Chapter 2.

Chapter 3 will take up the theme of culture, with special reference to sexuality as being at the core of cultural formation in birth, the family, and human relationships. Political and legal usages vitally impinge on all these, leading in Chapter 4 to a discussion of the shape of the religious mind as perpetuated in, but necessarily responsive to, the vagaries of time and the flux of centuries. How equipped are the faiths to cope with secular dilemmas, and out of what resources can they respond? Attitudes and capacities of religious leadership are at issue here as well as the vested interests inherent in traditional authority. How resilient are faiths calculated to be, both in discerning their problems wisely and in guiding their communities effectively?

That any continuing sense of Christian mission has to measure rightly all the foregoing must be obvious. Traditional ideas of mission have been in crisis this half century. Chapter 5 considers the following: How does the vocation look today? In what terms can Christian finality hold in the climate of secular irreligion, the gathering pluralism of cultural awareness, and the competition, even within dialogue, of distinctive "authorities" of revelation? The Christian church is present in every culture, but it has heavy traditional liaison with the hemisphere whence contemporary secularity in large measure derives. If Christianity has longer experience, it also has larger debts. Will it be possible to think of mission to other faiths as such, rather than simply as a will to recruiting from them by personal conversion? If so, how?

The conviction that it must be "mission with the God of patience" seems to follow powerfully from the perceptions with which we began, in the negligibility of God and the secular inconsequentiality of divine transcendence. If these are as we read them, and if God is indeed God, there must be a "woundedness" in the divine nature, an infinite readiness to be self-finited even to the point of being ignored in his own creation. Is it not precisely this that the Christian faith has always known as the long-suffering evidence of the divine earnestness?

2

The Realm of Politics and Law

Incognito ergo sum[1] has sometimes been suggested as a wryly appropriate divine comment about secularity: "I am in being unknown." It was noted in Chapter 1 that the human experience of God is often casual, if not unwanted. It is one thing that atheism denies the reality of God, another that secularity ignores it. These are different ways of saying along with the people whom Isaiah the prophet knew: "Let us hear no more... cause the Holy One of Israel to cease from among us" (30:10–11). There is the demand for explicit disavowal, and there is the habit of idle indifference. The God we deny may find apologists; the God we ignore is left to a limbo that has no call for apologists.

It follows either way, but urgently in the second case, that religious conviction concerning God, however named, should be "established"; that is, it should have sustained social and cultural "evidences"—in rite, community, and institutional being. These state the claim and plead the cause. They are custodians in the custody

of what the religion means and intends, of how it inter-
prets and proposes to organize the world. They are
declarative and performative concerning the being of
Yahweh, or Allah, or God-in-Christ, or diversely of deity
in human cognizance.

Secularity, or secularization, if we do not distinguish
the terms, clearly neglects, disparages, or decries these
institutionalized forms of the meanings they house, even
as it doubts or dismisses the meanings themselves.
Clearly, the meanings and the means to them have a
common life, and for good or ill, share a common for-
tune. As we must see, it is possible for a conformity to
stay with the forms when the heart has gone out of the
things they inform. That phenomenon is a large part of
the perplexity that secularity holds for the devout and
the believing. Even so, in due course, the expressions
will go where the convictions went, if these have passed
into agnostic decay.

The security of these necessary religious establishments and of the faiths enshrined in them has been
almost universally sought in identifying both belief and
structure with ethnic identity, national solidarity, and
state-power. All religions show clear proofs of this
instinct to incorporate believing and to believe in incorporation. Language, territory, and demography of course
contribute enormously to this instinctive solidarity in
religion. Its durability is evident throughout history. It is
the major preoccupation of relationships in dialogue.
Identity confers meaning, and meaning indwells identity. The Sikh simply is the Sikh, the Muslim the Muslim,
the Jew the Jew, and all their distinctive selves, even
though secularity may have induced great disparities
inside the several establishments.

The early Christians might seem to have been set for a significant exception, bound over as they were to a Messiah who saved them from sin, not from Roman subjugation; a Messiah by virtue not of a successful Masada, but of a Golgotha. Their mandate to the world proved itself a kingdom open to all believers, belief being an option in no way precluded by birth, race, speech, or culture. Nevertheless, after three suffering centuries, the Empire took over the church. Constantine's concern, via the Council of Nicaea, for uniform agreement on doctrine, and his amalgam of faith and rule in a Christus Imperator, stemmed directly from the imperial tradition that the state required divine acknowledgment from all and sundry. The old Rome had tolerated sects, on condition of emperor worship, because it was indifferent to what sectarian deities might otherwise signify. As committed to God alone, to "the Lord who is One," the first Christians could not accede to that Roman thesis. When, under Constantine, the Empire became God's patron, it would still demand a politically Roman form of the new monotheism, one fused into the power equation.

Thus was inaugurated the long Christian marriage of state and faith. Julian the Apostate's brief reversion to the old order did not long disrupt it. Constantine was at length renewed in Charlemagne and the (Western) Holy Roman Empire. Byzantium sustained its own Eastern form of Christ and power. When Christendom broke into nation-states in the wake of the Renaissance and the Reformation, these emulated the same instincts. The incidence of those events tended strongly to identify the shape of Christianity with power forms, as in Catholic Spain, the Protestant Netherlands, and Anglican-Elizabethan England. The wrong religious affiliation was a form of treason because the situation was reciprocal. How could recusants and papists make good an English patriotism in the days of the Spanish Armada's calculated invasion of England with a view to ensuring a Roman Catholic version of the English state?

These historical definitions coinciding religious and national loyalties together are well enough known to need no detailed exegesis here, except to say that Christianity had once been quite otherwise. As a persecuted minority, it was adopted by no regime and was under grievous suspicion by the only pagan one there was. Thus there is nothing inherently Christian in the state connection, as either the due or the only form of being duly godly in the world. Even when seekers after liberty, from the Anglican establishment and/or Roman Catholic power, emigrated to the new world in Massachusetts or Virginia, they took with them their own version of believing citizens and citizen-believers. "Freedom to worship God" was not yet freedom from their version of its right auspices.

The case with Islam was different *ab initio.*[2] Muhammad being, as it were, his own Constantine (*mutatis mutandis*). The post-Hijrah Islamic "establishment" at Yathrib (Medina) was an amalgam of faith and power so strong that apostasy from the one was treason to the other. Submission to divine revelation meant submission to its power expression in the *Ummah* and *Dawlah* of Islam. Indeed, the latter might precede the former. There is an intriguing passage in Surah 49.14 of the Qur'an in which some desert Arabs came to Muhammad after his conquest of Mecca, saying: "We have believed." He was directed to tell them:

> You have not believed: you should rather say: "We
> have surrendered" (or "...Have become Muslims").
> Faith has not entered your hearts. If you obey
> God and His messenger, He will not let you forfeit
> any of your deeds.[3]

Real believing could no doubt follow, reinforced by the
evident success of Muslim power.[4] Whatever the order,
the two parts of one equation are clear.

It was the same under Islamic expansion, which
was essentially a military, imperial thing.[5] It gave the
option to Jews and Christians of remaining so, though
the sanctions, economic and personal, against doing so
were formidable. Islam was not spread by the sword (as
ignorance has it); it was spread as an empire, and those
who Islamized did so having been conquered. The sanction was power in concert with preaching.[6] Islam was
thus the most political of all the great religions, and that
without inhibition or any sense of compromise. Indeed,
the logic of Muhammad's Hijrah was precisely the legitimacy of religious power and the powered legitimacy of
religion. The ensuing centuries perpetuated that conviction by the institution of the caliphate. Its vicissitudes have been many, and it has now since 1924
given way to a divided *Ummah* and the separate nation-
state. What still remains mandatory to the Islamic
mind is that this religious faith assumes, desires, and
proceeds by state-and-power expression.

The creation of Pakistan in the 1940s was the clear-
est demonstration of this instinctive perception. Despite
the enormous cost in life and misery, the die was cast
for a separate Muslim state where Muslim population
predominated. Illogical in that it condemned Muslims

elsewhere to permanent impossibility of Islamic state-hood, it was seen, however, as a sine qua non of survival at all by Pakistan. Permanent minority status in a United India was ruled out except by a brave minority of deeply Islamic thinkers, despite all the human factors urging it.[7]

Hinduism in India after partition might well have been provoked by the logic of Pakistan to declare a Hindustan. Nehru-style secularism has, thus far, precluded that. By its own classic doctrine of caste, Hinduism fuses creed and society in its own thorough terms, so that the identity between India and Hindu religion abides within the constitution of a secular state.

Another example is the state of Israel. In the form of political Zionism, Judaism found statehood an authentic necessity despite the long centuries of a different authenticity in diaspora.[8] Jewish statehood remains, however, a massive contradiction in terms, inasmuch as its founding concepts were essentially secular; but, thanks to political constraints, its religio-legal patterns are sharply theocratic.

ii

The foregoing does scant justice to deep issues and long stories. Its point is simply that this ancient and persist-ing, if varying, politico-national structure of religion can be secularized in the legal sense without that in any nec-essary way implying or requiring secular abandonment of religious belief, ritual, and practice. It has already been stressed that the secular state concept can, and should, be emphatically distinguished from any making irreligious of society. It is entirely valid to combine a sys-tem in which the state is neutral in respect to freedom and faith-allegiance, with some continuing tradition of faith, worship, and religion.

There is a sense in which this means that religion becomes both private and an option. There are mentalities that see this as compromise, risk, attenuation of truth, or even as betrayal. It need be none of these. Indeed, the liberty of allegiance can serve also to purify or deepen the quality of faith itself by dint of being no longer protected, assumed, or enforced. Nor need it be supposed that to have the state no longer requiring and safeguarding a religion means that the state itself is no longer accountable to, or liable about, the obligations of justice and probity in public affairs.

The secular state in this sense of the word secular means no necessary abandonment of the Islamic principle that "religion extends over all life" and that *Al-Mulk lil-Lah,* "the sovereignty is God's," is a principle that Jews and Christians equally avow. The issue concerning such divine sovereignty is never *whether;* it is always *how.* There will remain whole areas of law and life necessarily subject to the criteria of the divine will as explicit or implicit in the scriptures of the faiths. In respect of justice, public order, ethical standards, and equality before the law, these sources of guidance and obligation will continue to influence, but the faith that informs them and undergirds their application will be the truer for its uncomplicated inwardness in the personal mind and heart.

Two practical factors point to this essentially spiritual perception of what religion is and does. One is the intermixing of two or more religions in the same body politic. The other is the interliability of all religions vis-à-vis human rights and international law as embodied in

the United Nations Charter and its institutional implementation.

Nations like Saudi Arabia, dominated and denominat-
ed almost totally by one religion, are few and will become
ever fewer. In numerous nations, particularly in Africa,
Muslims and Christians share common nationhood.
Asian states are full of minority communities, while in
Europe there have come to be large, resident, Western-
indigenized expressions of Asian faiths. For the Muslims
among them, statehood in separatist Islamic shape will
never be their option. Their Islam has, of necessity, to
be a personal confession, fulfilled in privately communal
ritual and translated into public law, order, and authority
only in terms of equal participation with other citizens
under a constitution not unilaterally identified with Islam
but derived from another tradition of faith and freedom.

In that sense Muslims in Britain, Holland, Germany,
and elsewhere in Europe are *already* effectively de-
Islamized, if Islam is defined in old caliphal terms under
which Muslims must never be ruled by non-Muslims and
could, therefore, not tolerate any government, democ-
racy, régime that shared power outside their faith identity. It is wise, therefore, to have ideology overtaking
this actual situation by defining a version of Islam in
which—in that hitherto unthinkable Western phrase—
it is "just a religion." There are welcome signs that this
is happening.[9] For the multitude of diaspora Muslims,
old concepts of *Dar al-Islam* and *Jihad* have become
physically untenable. They can now, in these fields,
have only a spiritual, and therefore personal, relevance
and be effectively political only in cooperation with non-
Muslims. To remain theocratic, antisecular, caliphal, or
power-girt, in the old terms, is no longer feasible or

intelligible. What used to be the sine qua non of classical Islam has now become, if persisted in, its *cum qua non.*

The realization that this is so can be very salutary. It is by no means a misfortune, or a situation for dismay, for reasons that are better discussed in Chapter 4. Given a secular state, the resources of minorities can be tested in cooperation. At least in Western societies, deep issues are emerging around what might be called "civil religion." On whom does the president of the United States call for an invocation at the inauguration? How does the British Commonwealth of Nations express "commonweal" in interreligious terms when occasions require? In towns and villages there are times of public celebration, corporate significance, school ceremony, and the like, all calling for some measure of interfaith participation.

Israel was so named because not all its population would be Jews.[10] Would there be any place for a non-Judaic spirituality? The question has proved very painful because, for deep historical reasons, the new state was conceived in determination to be passionately Jewish. The shape of that passion is still urgently in contention.

On every count, everywhere, secularity *qua* state (firmly distinguished from secularity as total) confronts both majority and minority elements with sharp tests. How far are the former ready for the loosening of state ties lately uniquely theirs? How far are the latter ready for genuine participation with the self-searching and self-risking this entails? The ghetto was the traditional refuge of minority minds when state-faith was regnant. It is a mentality hard to forsake, raising always the quandary around mutual trust. The Enlightenment in nineteenth-century Europe wooed many in Jewry out of

the ghetto into fully-fledged Germanism, only to be desperately betrayed in the twentieth. Political Zionism
then passed its aggressive verdict on the perpetual inca-
pacity of the "Gentile" world for honesty, its anti-
Semitism being perceived as inveterate. Ghettoes have
a perennial appeal, and secular states must recognize in
them their deepest interrogation.

Are minorities willing to belong? Is the secular state
dependably neutral? The answers rest with the
resilience of the faiths inside the equations, both
minority and traditional. To pass muster we might say,
in a sort of paradox, that the truly secular state needs to
be carefully spiritual. Ghettoes can be mentally perpetuated when no longer physically expressed. Culture looms as
a threatening factor. Genuine religious-mindedness
needs to move from old and into new parameters of
behavior and association. The flux of generations may
facilitate but also embitter the process. How is assimi-
lation loyal both to past and to future? What new perspectives in old faiths are legitimate and sound? Who
is to say?

As for majority faiths, the question must be whether
they can rise to honest reckoning with secular neutrality and wisely retain their sense of liability for long
national tradition. Militant Islam will not even raise the
question, for its statehoods refuse to be secular. An
Islam or a Judaism negotiating wisely with itself might
be ready to do so. The case made here is that a single
religion could properly continue to play the major role
in the spirituality of secular statehood, on condition that
it respected and recruited the contribution of faiths present in the body politic but not hitherto sharing its historic definition or its cultural assumptions. The sense in

which Europe and Christianity interdefine—as do India and Hinduism; Pakistan, Arab lands, and Islam; the United States and its European sources of ideology—seems to make this case self-evident on every ground. The permutations are endless. But in broad terms, language, history, and culture combine to condition the secular state, both as concept and as legal fact, so that a tradition of religion characterizes its very capacity to be organized in secular terms. That it might continue to do so seems self-evident on every ground of practicality and desirability.

It is germane to this argument that we question a too facile way of talking about "multiculture." This term almost spells a contradiction. Identities are not merged like mountain streams into one river. Nor are they mergeable. They are rivers in themselves. We miss the whole theme of compatibility if we think it merely happening. History is too tough a dimension of existence. Secularity, we have been arguing, *qua* statehood is not indifference. Nor can the concepts that underwrite legal freedoms, cultural expression, social integration be divorced from the ultimate custody they have found—or failed to find—in received religions. The entire case for the secular state presupposes an alerting, not a deposing, of faith liability.

The alerting has to do with a necessary humility, a quality of mind and spirit that marries conviction with tolerance and is ready to conceive of civil partnerships beyond its own creed, on condition of reciprocal readiness. Party political debate is an obvious example in contrast to ghetto apathy or exclusively sectarian politics. In the United States, the Constitution excludes religious affiliation from national reckonings; yet the population, by tradition, has been observant in its several worships. There the historic factors are almost *sui generis.*

The current British situation presents a different paradigm. Having a long enduring "Establishment" with bishops by right in the Upper House of Parliament (and Anglican clergy debarred from election into the Lower), the Church *of* England has long wanted to incorporate the churches in England into that trusteeship. Now there is the larger question of the place in British spirituality of Jews, Muslims, Hindus, Sikhs, Bahais, and others. Were there not the historic Establishment, it would now be anachronistic to create it. But having it, to terminate it could signify that the state is a law to itself and not "this orb set under the Cross."[11] That would mean either a total secularity or a legal secularity in which its own law was its own absolute, causing it thereby to cease to be even a secular state in terms we have here made mandatory. We are a long way from Richard Hooker's Ecclesiastical Polity and from Edmund Burke's version of "No Church, no state,"[12] yet we are not saying with Voltaire: "...Écrasez l'infâme."

In a secularity of participant, but historically unequal, faiths (in respect of their present incidence), all faiths are put on their mettle—the dominant ones to rethink their dominance, the minority ones their timidity, their martyr complex, or their resentments. The quality of such rethinkings will obviously be reciprocal, the risks different but mutual, the inhibitions crucial.

iii

Deferring discussion of the resources available for these demands to Chapter 4, it could be illuminating to study briefly the secular experience of God in the state of Israel.

On the one hand, we have in its creation what some would see as the greatest fact of the twentieth century; on the other, a sharp example of a secular state thoroughly nonsecular in its legal framework. To be sure, there are Israelis who are not Jews, that is, Arabs, and—in the eyes of the Rabbinate—"non-Jewish Jews." The paradox arises from the politics of state creation as a strenuous and entirely comprehensible demand to end the diaspora status of Jewry and to embody Jewish ethnicity securely in a state-nation, recovering the tradition of David and the Maccabees and forever settling—in both ideological and physical senses of the word—Judaic identity. The state demanded to be, therefore, conceptually homogenous, despite "the existing population."[13]

The state created was thus, in one sense, a neutrally secular entity. Far from coming, like those nations we have been discussing, into any even tenuous interreligious compatibility, it existed in sharply definitive, even defiantly distinctive, Jewish terms. Those nations were coming reluctantly and painfully *out* of religious exclusivity; Israel was ardently entering *into* it by urgent logic of long Jewish suffering under the frequent exclusivity of other nations. It even took some of its logic from that "Gentile" ideology.[14] Doing so, it was deliberately repudiating—against the grain of its finest diaspora perceptions—the inclusivity of humankind, the relativity of national human denominators, for Zionism perceived that inclusivity as a mirage.

The paradox deepens in that, although the initiation was secular in the souls of Herzl, Nordau, Weizmann, Ben-Gurion, and their compatriots, the implementation—thanks to political vicissitudes under the Israeli

Constitution—made the law of society rigorously reli-
gious in its statements on birth, marriage, and legal
"Jewishness" in these terms. By differing criteria, the
Israeli Jewish citizen was at once Jewish and not Jewish.
The Sabbath has been a sharp point at issue in this
equation—witness the contrast between the beaches of
Tel Aviv and the streets of Mea Shearim.

All has, of course, been tragically conditioned by the
Palestinian presence. Although the ideal of homogeneity
might require negotiation and a compatibility drawn on
the map, the urge for security demanded the totality of
territory and anathema on partition. Internal to all this
lies the ever-vexed issue of how "the holy" is duly moral
and the moral properly "holy." All is still *sub judice* in
the soul and conscience of the participants and may
well forever remain so.

No analysis is here intended, elusive as all analysis
must be. The sole point of concern is to see how the
state of Israel enshrines, for good or ill, the most insistent issues that wait on secular nationhood. Perhaps all
is incredibly entangled because it has to do with what is,
ostensibly, "the holy land." Zionism is impaled on the
enigma of holiness itself, on whether any land can ever
possess it or give it political expression. Israel, therefore,
uniquely and acutely undergoes a paradox at the core of
its being. For Israelis outside Orthodox Judaism, Israel
offers a provocative secular experience of God at every
wedding and on every Sabbath; and to the devout at
Torah ritual, a secular experience of his betrayal.

iv

The concept of some collaboration between faiths in the
reading of social problems and the addressing of them in

legislation and in the debates concerning it, if com-
bined, as suggested, with a continuing hegemony for a
predominant faith, will make strenuous demands on
all. The doctrinal aspects will come under "the shape of
the religious mind." However, the shape of the religious
structure will also be vital. Communities have vested
interests, as also do their mentors, in rite and doctrine.
Shaikhs and mullahs, rabbis and clerics enjoy a certain
prestige that hinges on their stake in beliefs and rituals.
If the enterprise needs humility in practice, it needs it
too in practitioners. Among them it may be far to seek.

One hope of coming by it may lie in the realization
that the areas in which religious decisions are required
are increasingly shared, being global. The old isolations of
faiths are at an end. Minorities here are majorities
there—across sometimes adjacent borders. "Take care of
ours and we will take care of yours" can then be sound
pragmatism, far better than a precarious hostage system,
but it will be well to have it sanctioned in international
law, binding on all states. The United Nations already has
that authority. The concept of "a law of nations" obviously cuts across self-sufficiency and can stimulate separate
dogmas to align their perceptions. The claims of feminism have the same logic.[15] Meanwhile the reality of
technology without frontiers—except the drastic economic ones—confronts all faith adherence in varying degrees
of common secular experience. That fact, having termi-
nated a local isolation, may also end an intellectual one.

There are many issues here to be remitted to later
pages. My hope is that the case is clearly made for a secular politics in legal form that in no way necessitates or
even anticipates an overall irreligion. Faith may be no
less, perhaps far more, authentic for being a personal

option, nevertheless relevant in freedom to the social order and to the nation at large. That it may not be, that it may wilt and wither for lack of power status and state-aegis, remains an open question. Outright seculariza-tion, the relinquishment of transcendent reference, is— as the poet might have said—in "the tides of time." The sacred, however, will always remain the destiny of the secular and the secular the raw material of the sacred. There is no frontier between them. When Jesus said to a questioner about God and Caesar: "Render to God the things that are God's and to Caesar what is Caesar's," he did not speak of division but of interpenetration (cf. Hinchliff 1982; Warren 1955). Caesar had no autonomy outside divine sovereignty, nor was divine sovereignty excluded from Caesar's realm. The secular state, rightly conceived, means no abdication of the sacred. If it were so to mean, it could hardly even be secular.

Concluding so, we are bound to ask: What resilience do the faiths have to fulfill their meaning, acknowledg-ing this version of business with the world? A prior question takes us first beyond politics and law to a cru-cial theme of humankind in every culture.

3

The Theme in Sex and Culture

There is nothing that so privatizes human experience as sexual exchange, yet nothing that so crucially belongs with the social scene: with time past, by heredity; with time future, via progeny; and with time present, in partnership and family. In sex we may experience the inherent sacrament of personhood or engage in the worst trivialization of our meaning. In sexuality, nature and nurture most intimately meet to yield the first elements of culture.

In the previous chapter we saw that the entire field of secularity, or secularization (if we use those terms interchangeably), requires a necessary distinction: between "secular" as describing a state or society in which religious allegiance might freely vary within a common citizenship and share common civil and political rights equally, and "secular" denoting a condition or attitude of mind that rejects or ignores divine transcendent reference altogether, saying or implying that there is only us, only human referents for human referees.

The former meaning concerned us earlier. The present task is with the second. Of course, the two may well coexist. To have faith be a matter of indifference before the law may leave it a matter of indifference *in toto*. If how or whether I worship, pray, or revere is immaterial to the state, maybe it is immaterial altogether. What is left in my option in state-polity may come to be optional altogether. Such total optionality has no room for "Thus says the Lord" and mightily conflicts with *Allahu akbar*. It is evident, on all hands, that religious faiths have either established "cities of God" or assumed them explicit in any "God of cities." Foregoing any state-connected privilege is a large part of the testing of religions today, their caliber of mind, their capacity of spirit. To be and to serve, without benefit of any sanction but their own worth of meaning and wealth of heart, test religions even more radically than did conditions of political empowerment.

Our earlier reflections on the secular state have to be taken forward into this chapter's duty to inclusive secularity. The causes and sources of secularity in the last two centuries, mainly in the West, have often been analyzed. Creeds and religions in historical expression have dismayed careful minds, their truths sometimes seeming like conspiracies of silence around awkward questions. Theologies seem often in retreat, with rearguard actions about a geocentric universe, or the nature of miracle, or the story of man, or the authority of Scriptures, or the body-soul equation. Credence and credibility have often seemed at odds. Hearts have sickened in dismay in suspicion of hypocrisy, self-deceit, or the vested interests of prestige.

Any such impulses to agnosticism have been further

sharpened by the perpetual renewal of the ancient problem of tragic wrong: the suffering of the innocent, the prosperity of the guilty, the impossibility of explicit ethics in such a world, and endless reproductions of the old conundrum of an almighty power that lacks the will, or an almighty will that lacks the power. To have both power and love in one seems a futile delusion. The conclusion presses that any theological assurance as to divine love has no foundation but its own wishfulness. Once this is realized it becomes the duty of honesty to renounce the self-deception. Others would say *denounce,* having no compunction about "Lampe needing his God," as Immanuel Kant commented about his gardener. If theism is allowed to survive, it can only be as consolation to the gullible.

These varied sources of secular skepticism belong, of course, with the intoxications of applied science, the multiplying achievements of technology. These make the old reliance on prayer and divine mystery now seem invalid. There is a recession in the sense of God contingent on an obsession with the sufficiencies that are our own. "Techniques" displace providence. Even our great menaces in the nuclear cloud or Internet are manmade. The world that used to be wonderful to shepherds pondering the night sky need no longer be so to astronauts, or so it seems.

Further, because "the proper study of mankind is man," the exploration of the psyche and of society have yielded psychology and sociology as "techniques" for both. One result has been to reduce experience to the particulars of phenomena. The rituals and desires of religion become a special target here. Sociologists do well, indeed, to note and probe precisely how people "behave" and how things "proceed." This may yield useful clues about how to advertise. Practical studies can be "value-free" in the sense that they are pursued, disinterestedly, just to discover how they operate, whether it be people in love (or hate) or habits in sanctuaries.

What is legitimate here readily gravitates, however, into everything becoming value-free altogether, just functional, observable as a phenomenon but not significant in reality. The implication is quite lethal to any sense of the transcendent. Intelligent Islamic writing, for example, has been very alert to the implications of sociological reductionism in these areas. Anxious about the evisceration of truth-concepts and the impact of sociology in higher education, it has developed a new form of its classic self-sufficiency by demanding and aiming to supply a complete "Islamicization of knowledge" (see, e.g., al-Faruqi 1982 and Sardar 1985). This means that the firm framework of Quranic revelation has to be the sufficient touchstone of all truth and the explicit presupposition of all right knowing.

It is an unfortunate and shortsighted reaction, but it constitutes a sobering measure of how inimical to religious faith the exclusifying of scientific criteria of meaning and reality can be. Christian responses have not needed, for reasons that may be clearer in the next chapter, to resort to any overall Christianization of knowledge. It is clear that sciences and techniques ignore religious frontiers. There is no Judaic biology, no Christian aeronautics, no Muslim chemistry, but only experts from any tradition exercising scientific skills indifferently.

It is impossible to be exhaustive here about the sources and causes of total secularity. What is important must be the personal consequences in individuals and societies. One might almost say that the consequence in broad terms is inconsequentiality. Certainly the literature, novels, plays, and poetry of the secular time witness to this quality. "Our lot is intermittence," wrote Marcel Proust, making it the motif of the longest novel with the sparsest action. As Roger Shattuck said of Proust:

> He undermines individual character as the source of anything coherent or reliable in our behaviour. Love, friendship, honesty and sexuality crumble into mockery of human relationships (1974:12).

Virginia Woolf's perceptive diaries and novels explore poignantly a personal world that she advised to "give things their caricature value" (1980:3:203). In his story about an actress, Thornton Wilder wrote:

> As her technique became sounder her sincerity became less necessary. Even when she was absent-minded the audience did not notice the difference (1927:80–81).

Overall technique—scientific, behavioral, social— has somehow dethroned sincerity, but we seculars desperately notice the difference and ask what has happened to us at the hands of those who have "taken away [ourselves] and we know not where [they are] laid." This is secularity.

Pleading for "real words for honest ends," the English playwright Dennis Potter talks of a "ludicrous plight… to be kept under properly contemptuous control." He adds:

> We live in a society that is ruled by an occupying power (pushing) us all to an impotent acceptance,

the entropy of a culture under alien rule… a
people only half conscious of their subjection
(1984:4, 24).

Does language allow us any possibility to mean? Has
meaning any intelligible language?

ii

The secularity of sexuality is plainly the central focus of
this elusive, perhaps illusionary, selfhood. It deserves, as
here, to represent the whole. It is in the realm of the loss
of frames of moral reference, or religious perspectives
and hallowing instinct, that the secular casualties of the
casual belong, and belong most cruelly. A sardonic story
by Nathanael West (1993) may capture things at issue.
It has to do with a male writer on the *New York Post*
who takes on the job of answering readers' letters under
the caption "Miss Lonelyhearts." The assignment is considered a joke, but he accepts hopefully en route to
something better in journalism. After several months
the notion of a joke pales. Most letters turn out to be
from desperate, lovesick, love-battered, wistful, angry,
perplexed people seeking answers. He is disturbed to
find that correspondents take him seriously. As never
before, he is compelled to examine what values there
may be. He becomes the final victim of the joke. The letters are in no way funny. He finds he is responding with
sentimental rubbish. The column closes down, and with
it, a redundant pseudo-moralist.

One might say that most things secular are here: The
trivial unable to be serious; the serious lost in triviality;
make-believe about belief; the pseudo where the true
should be; and, with all these, the groping of the human

quest, the ill-directed search for meaning, the bankrupt-cy of where the quest turns.

There is hardly need in present context to list the fea-tures of the contemporary culture of sexuality or the pre-cise role of technology, the linguistic philosophers, the sundry mentors in the arts, advertisement, and drama, in our arriving at where we are. Certainly techniques of contraception, of fertility, and of abortion have radically altered the perspectives of sexual activity, of gender roles in society, and of perceptions of personality itself. The media have massively contributed to a climate of sexual matters as private affairs, transactions feasibly separable from religious norms or social concern. Preoccupation with the physical aspects of sex has totally ousted the old restraints that once made it the "silent" subject (which death has now become). The metaphysics of mystery and wonder have been lost in the commercial, the triv-ial, the transient, and the vulgar.

The consequences are enormous in the uncertain loyalties of one to another, of parent to child, of each to any. We suffer the moral detritus of broken homes, deprived or depraved families, and coarsened relation-ships. For some, reverence has come to seem the impo-sition of some code or killjoy rubric that deserves to be defied in the interests of liberty and life. Let no one be convicted of a creed or cramped by a code. Realism says that no one knows for sure about reality and no one is warranted to tell us.

There has been much in twentieth-century history with its vast wars and chronic tragedies to foster this conspiracy of consent to apathy, this battle at all costs—and unsuccessfully—with boredom. "We are such stuff as lusts are made of and our little life is bounded with a yawn." Unsure fundamentally about ourselves, let sex be simply a genital pursuit, our genders debatable or rebellious, our affairs private, and our souls adrift.

iii

How does a religious sense of mission relate to this impervious culture with a "no admission" on its heart? Only to condemn will not be mission. "Desist" will be only a partial call, for there is everything to be salvaged, retrieved, redeemed. We have not understood the vacancies and travesties if we have not known the real fulfillments and the true clothings of our nakedness. This entire theme of having a right sexuality is a large part of the proper interconcern of the religions.

Buddhism, of course, in its sharper forms, finds itself confirmed in its will to the atrophy of sexual desire per se. The drive of our being has to be known for the renunciation it must teach. That solution may forgo and forfeit love in the very repudiation of lust.

Islam exemplifies the place of law but often misses its incompleteness. Sexuality in Islam duly presupposes contractual status for the parties. This is so even in *muta'*, or transient marriage. Divorce is permitted but hateful; and discarded wives have legal rights. Promiscuity, scorning legal forms, is reprehensible. Other theisms, too, think of marriage as a proper legal shape to sexuality, in pledge and tie. This is, however, a potential negativity that hardly responds to the climate we have noted. The habit of the veil may be seen as a sorry verdict on the capacity of the masculine in society for self-control, for tenderness and singleminded loyalty. The old harem was a licensed potential for lust. That current Muslim feminism has an authentic mission and a strenuous journey cannot be in doubt.

The Christian sexual vision must be honest with itself, being in measure responsible for the society that has—by other than Christian momentum—spawned the sexual panorama we perceive around us. Such honesty, however, need have no reticence about its essential reading of the physicality of human love. Christianity reads it as a sacrament. The term is the core of any body/spirit, and flesh/troth equation. It is, therefore, the clue—in any sphere—of how we must comprehend the sacred and the secular.

It is the nature of the sacrament to "mean in doing" and to "do in meaning." Action transacts and meaning inheres. More than merely denoting or informing like signposts, sacraments both tell and convey. Thus an embrace, a kiss, a gift, a salute, a handshake, a smile or frown are "telling" things. They recruit sense to make sense. They make meaning both perceptible and tangible so that, we might say, "it happens."

Sexual exchange is of this order, supremely. Physically it necessitates entire personal reciprocal imparting, exposure, donation, and reception—a unison of participation. Christian sense of the sacrament accepts it so, as the consecration of personality, given and received. As such, it means loyalty and seeks perpetuation. This, and not some mere legality, is what Christian marriage, as sacramental, hallows and fulfills; hence the commitment and the fidelity that properly possess it. Ever to have transacted love in these terms is to know how authentically abiding its nature is; hence the urgency of these perspectives for its antecedents.

It is precisely this theology of sexuality that releases
the compassion and redemptiveness that have to greet
its breakdowns and its betrayals. The sanctity and the
redemption have to be held together. The sacramental is
not its true self if it makes human persons the tragic vic-
tims of its meaning, for it originates in the grace of God.
There will always be a necessity to hold together the twin
truths of divinely meant sacramental love in couples,
homes, and families, and of divinely meant fulfillment,
beyond frailty and guilt, of personalities in grace.

Is love therefore to be confined to marriage, some will
ask? Love, apart from physical sexual expression, is of
course on every hand in friendship and society. One of
the tragedies of insistent sexual physicality is that the
obsession jeopardizes generous friendliness everywhere.
It propels adolescents into self-doubt or troublous anxiety at the very point when they need to discover what all
things mean and do so without pressure to conform to
vulgar, unthinking assumptions.

How can the sacramental principle, it will be asked,
obtain in same-sex situations of friendship, mutual
interest, and shared activity at work, in sport, or anywhere? Must these be excluded from the physicality
that sacramental faith itself holds is authentically right?
Faith must be its own mentor here and not turn only on
Levitical precept. There is much confusion. We need in
this world all the love we can come by, but in terms consistent with love's meaning.

In homosexuality there is always a certain sterility
and often a deep evasiveness, putting a question mark
around any reciprocal gratitude for our own place in
the generations. That apart, there is also much confusion about the vexed question of whether a homosexual

condition is a "given," like color blindness, a tendency to baldness, or brown eyes. What is "natural" will always beg endless questions. Certainly it is not the least difficult to visualize mutual masturbation between those of one gender. That ability, unless disciplined by some sacramental sense, readily engenders much nonconsenting abuse. Such abuse, of course, is in no way confined to homosexuals. Heterosexuals are no less prone to rape, exploitation, prostitution, and sodomy.

Either way, the ultimate criterion belongs with the sense of sex as sacrament. That genuine intermale, interfemale companionship can or should be supposed or required to be inherently genital in order to be either sincere or satisfactory is manifestly obscene and profane. There is much hypocrisy in the zeal for "outing" individuals on the easy assumption of their being hypocrites in any and every friendship between the same genders. Ambiguity may be as much a mirage of the suspicious as a refuge of the perplexed. Certainly the capacity for platonic friendships is too precious, both for society and for personhood, to have it gossiped into something needing to "come clean" when it already is so.[1]

The New Testament church grew and spread in a society prone, if not inured, to homosexual love in genital terms. Its answer lay in the hallowing of flesh and spirit as one, in the meaning the Incarnation had conferred on all physicality, namely, that the soul was a sanctuary and the body "a temple of God." As such, it was to be a "vessel of honor, meet for the Master's use" (2 Tim. 2:21; 1 Thess. 4:4). The Master was the Lord, yet also subordinately the self, as being the Lord's. The sacramental principle is not enforceable, though law

may administer it where the social will is present.
Sacramentality is an obedience of the will grounded in a
love of the divine.

iv

It can be seen also as the clue to an interpretation and
discipline of the several techniques of recent science
that have engendered new demands on conscience and
contributed massively to a culture of "management"
and "arrogance" in the most sensitive areas of life and
death. Artificial insemination, *in vitro* fertilization,
genetic engineering, scientific manipulation both of
birthing and of dying—all these are no more than developed reaches of human dominion, not divinely with-
drawn and not to be disinvented. Yet dominion was
entrusted to creatures and creaturehood its tributary,
commissioned to be its own mentor with the restraints
on usurpation internal to its own responsible mind.
Thus the sense of the sacramental has to come into the
laboratory and the research houses to ensure that all
our capacities are accountable and that the humanity
wielding them is the humanity governing them in a gov-
ernance that is only right when sacramental. For our
mastery is our "secular experience of God"—of God, not
a figment of our usurpation, but the Lord of our obedience and love, the Master of our mastery in his name.

The culture of management and techniques that is
dominant everywhere does interesting things to the
whole concept of what culture is. What used to be central to culture was its bewilderingly plural forms.
Climatic, ethnic, hereditary, and geographical factors
contributed to endless diversity—a diversity perpetuated
by isolation, distance, ignorance, and tribal mythology.

In their plural shapes, cultures were dedicated to the preservation and assertion of identity—identity in which sexual capacity and usages played a central part. Hence the new globalism, coinciding with the coming of new techniques in the sexual field, has had a sharp impact on population, copulation, gender roles, the family and, via all these, human meaning itself.

"The culture of techniques" is plainly ubiquitous. The appetite for technology is everywhere, though the economic disparities mean accentuated cultural tensions posed by identities countering as well as absorbing the new situation. In the face of "Pepsicolonization" and all its works, human diversity suffers a "sea change" that approximates all to certain common denominators. These are made the more incisive because of the imbalance in their incidence in history. The culture of techniques, of radio and television, of mass media and airports, of instantaneous information and the terrestrial significance of space exploration, presses hard upon traditional cultures that are striving for appropriate perpetuation under the perceived threat of ineluctable change.

In this sense they are all undergoing a "secular experience of *God*," if by God we can, for the time being, denote all that by myth, ritual, and ethnic patronage has been the referent of their meaning and their continuity. The major religions are a large domain of this reference, by which relatedness to the divine has been understood and practiced.

Study of this aspect belongs with the following chapter, but we might preface it by asking whether—as some theorists now hold—there is something genetic in cultures themselves, whether the religions informing them

are also seen as a sort of hereditary repository of attitudes, clues, and psychic determinants of thought that
provide the norms, rites, and codes by which cultures
are conscious of a collective self. Some agnostic minds
take this conjecture further and see religions-in-cultures
as genetically constituted "disease." The hypothesis
might then be invoked to explain the wrongs and evils
of religions' story: the wars, conflicts, persecutions, mal-
adies, bigotries, and hostilities of religions, abetting ethnic feuds and aiding human malice by endowing these
with divine sanction. "Secular experience of God" on
this assumption could only be a belated awakening to a
desperate condition from which, if at all, only a resolute,
aggressive secularity could ever hope to rescue us.

Such a view of culture *qua* religion could well seem
plausible from history. Freud has already made familiar
the notion of collective neurosis. Jeremiah long ago had
a burden for a society he perceived as "desperately sick"
and "deceitful above all things" (17:9). A fellow prophet
had seen paganism shaping for him this conclusion:

> A deceived heart has turned him aside so that he
> cannot deliver his soul nor say: "Is there not a lie
> in my right hand?" (Isa. 44:20).

Religion as genetic mischief and Hebraic prophethood
are very far apart, but together they may at least remind
us that there is even insanity in religious doings and that
religion is far from being always either a desirable or an
admirable commodity. The truth of this should not be
lost on dialogue.

However, the notion of "genetic collective lunacy"
cannot hold. If it did, there could be no ambition for a
"religion pure and undefiled," as James put it (1:27).

Were the condition real, it would be undetectable. *Corruptio optimi pessima.* Any Judaic, Christian, Islamic understanding of creation and creaturehood would instinctively incorporate what seem the evidences of any genetic "culturing" into their foundation faith in human meaning as genuinely, yet also riskily, entrusted with the things of God. Human dignity, for these faiths, inheres essentially in human frailty. Rather than surrender to futility, it is wiser to claim our humanity only in the context of the praise of God—God being, in Isaac Williams' lines:

> Disposer supreme, and judge of the earth
> Who choosest for Thine the weak and the poor,
> To frail earthen vessels and things of no worth,
> Entrusting Thy riches which aye shall endure.

So doing, in the words of the Qur'an (2.30f.), "He knew His own mind."

4

The Shape of the Religious Mind

i

"Come on my right hand, for this ear is deaf,"
Shakespeare (act 1, scene 2, line 213) has his Julius
Caesar say, though the advice was unnecessary in
Caesar's case. The colossus "bestriding the earth" was
not deaf at all. The playwright invented it to give power
a little human frailty. "Which is the hearing side?" we
might ask of the great religions across the world. In
respect of where the two preceding chapters have
brought us, there is much evidence that the great religions are hard of hearing. Fundamentalisms, as we puz-
zlingly call them, are patently unready for what they
need to hear.

The distinction we have been at pains to make
between secularity *qua* statehood and secularity altogether is easily discounted by the religious mind. Vested
interests, both of religious office and dogma, resist it as
threatening old securities of privileged status and prestige. The concepts of religious humility and coexistence
are seen as inimical to ancient authority, to sacrosanct

Scriptures, and to the subservience proper to ritualized truth. It is fair to say that the very stridency of fundamentalisms on many fronts is sufficient proof of how far the inroads of irreligion or corrosive worldliness have gone. In these quarters it is hard to woo the religious mind away from bigotry and obscurantism and gain a listening ear for wiser perceptions of truth, for saner counsels in the crisis. "Which is your good ear?" has to be the patient question.

The instinct in this chapter will be to explore what is at issue in religious fundamentalism by concentrating on the case of Islam, leaving some Christian dimensions of the phenomenon to the end of the chapter as a prelude to the next. Jewish fundamentalism is *sui generis,* as indeed they all are. It is deeply embroiled in the ambiguities of political Zionism and the tensions within the Israeli state. It is also textured by the inveterate Judaic instinct to define itself in terms of a humanity in perennial conspiracy against it. For reasons that will be apparent, a study of Muslim prepossessions about secularity in all its meanings can usefully illuminate what the religious issues are precisely by giving them such sharp and vivid focus.

ii

Islam might well exemplify "fundamentalism" as what religion is, but only if we read the word aright. In Western usage, the term implies a dogmatism that resists or fails to realize any obligation to doubt itself, being immersed in what it refuses to interrogate because it is beyond question. That usage implies that such faith *should* be self-critical and fails to be. The term does not fit Islam in that form. Islamic assurance is beyond that sort of rationale. The word *fundamental-ism* does not exist in Arabic,[1] and if it did, it could only mean what, in a sense, all Muslims are, namely, pos-sessed of final truth in definitive and institutionalized form. They are, we might say, *inherently* fundamentalist, by the factors we will enumerate, whereas what is gener-ally accused elsewhere is *culpably* nonfundamentalist.

This distinction is important, for much confusion prevails. Our task later will be to try to see whether the inherent fundamentalism of Islam can ever find itself also culpable. Meanwhile we have to understand extremists, aggressives, and fanatics as intensifying, mainly for political and psychological reasons, percep-tions that are implicit in the sane instincts of a quieter, more reverent Islam. It is fair to say that no great faith has more exacting dimensions to face in becoming com-patible with sincere interreligion and with the secular interrogation. Yet, as we must see, the situation is far from hopeless. The resources for being "liberal"—failing a better term—are present.

This inherent self-sufficiency, this robust self-rightness in Islam has many elements. It is inherently fundamental in being received as *al-Din 'ind-Allah al-Islam,* "God's own religion" (Surah 3.19). Surah 30.30 explains, further, that human nature and being *muslim*[2] are one. The word *fitrah* can be translated either as "nature" or "religion," that for which and in which God natured or fashioned humanity. It is thus that Islam is the religion God meant, duly and properly tailored to what humans are.[3]

This "appropriate" religion did not originate with Muhammad. His task was to give it final, ultimate, and institutionalized expression. Its essence was anticipated from the days of Adam and partially or prospectively formulated by all other prophets. Thus Abraham, Moses, David, Jesus, and many other lesser figures were all "muslims." This conviction means that Muslims do not need to heed other faiths with concern for disparity or genuine diversity. If these are present, they only indicate falsities that have diverged from the one truth these others should have affirmed. Insofar as they do not, then by the only yardstick there is, which is Islam's, they are disqualified. The Qur'an is both judge and jury.

This sense in Islam of being inherently what religion should be, and always only rightly was, is reinforced by warrant of the institutional form it attained in the *Sirah*, or career, of Muhammad, with whom it became authentically politicized. Islam is thoroughly linked with and vindicated by the political dimension, and this fact has always added to its assurance and helped to spread its wings. To be sure, Muhammad had been, strictly speaking, only a "preacher" for thirteen heroic years in Mecca.[4] Resistance and antagonism led him to seek and find political force via the Hijrah, or emigration, and skillful consolidation in the alternative city, Medina, whence after eight years of militancy, he was able to bring Mecca to surrender. This impressive physical success and its sequel in wide expansion confirmed Islam in the complete legitimacy of the power dimension. It provided accreditation of its finality and of Jihad as its proper form. This perfected what had been embryonic in the earlier militancies of Abraham, Moses, and David. It threw into contrast the loyal, but only ideal, achievement of the prophet Jesus. It gave to Islam the sanction of success. In the contemporary scene, it underwrites the extreme difficulty Muslims have of thinking of religion innocent of power or acquiescent about not monopolizing it.

Fragmentation in early Islam soon engendered
communities like the Shi'ah, who in minority weak-
ness were enabled to learn the lessons of a suffering
faith. Yet when occasions later came in success for
their vindication, the other lesson of Sunni success
was dominant. Sufism, or Islamic mysticism, may be
seen as an inner disavowal of belligerence and a sort of
minority verdict in a search for soul-devotion and a
gentle, Islamic "love to God." These minorities, however, have never superseded, in the very inner definitions
of Islam, the pattern determined—and Muslims would
insist vindicated—in the fabric of original Muslim history. We are always surely fundamentalist where faith
feels and knows no qualms.

Nor does the form and content of the Quranic
Scripture readily give rise to these. Indeed, the Islamic
perception of what their Scriptures are and how they
came to be theirs strongly corroborates the other factors
in finality. Surah 2 opens with "the Book in which there
is nothing dubious." Muhammad is understood to have
received the text as a secretary might take down a dic-
tated letter. Even in eternity, truth is thought of as
"inscribed on a preserved tablet" (85.23). Its contents
are mediated onto the Prophet's lips (not as ideas into
his mind, but already as words) whence they reach their
human audience, some of whom, as scribes, inscribe
them on parchment for subsequent recitation by the
faithful. Thus the very speech, *kalam,* the "wording" of
God passes into human currency by lip and page.

This concept of *wahy,* "revelation" or "inspiration,"
means a uniquely sacrosanct Scripture. Exegesis, to be
sure, has to attend to the occasions, the times and
places, of its serial mediation to Muhammad over

twenty-three years, from 609 to 632, but this scholarly duty proceeds only within the perception of its nature as literal and in Arabic, infallible. Though the Qur'an appeals frequently for *tadabbur,* or "understanding," it seeks it on its own terms. The concept of a verbal format for truth controls theology. The recitation is flawed by any "slip of the tongue"; lapses are attributed to Satanic malignity intruding. The sanctity of Quranic calligraphy powerfully confirms the oracular quality of revelation, of a Scripture that does not simply "hold" truth but totally "inscribes" it.

These several grounds of Islamic finality are fulfilled in its reassuringly structured *Ummah* and *Shari'ah,* its "unitary community" and its "sacred law." They have their efficacy in solidarity and habituation. The faith-confession, or *Shahadah,* is simplicity itself. "There is no deity except Allah." (No Chalcedonian subtlety here!) The five-times daily *Salat,* or prayer ritual, both habituates piety and transacts powerful solidarity. *Salat* may often be solo, but it is strongly corporate in that the *Qiblah,* or direction of prayer, focuses all on Mecca, while the left-right greeting at the end of each prayer session salutes the entire Muslim community. Further, on Fridays, congregational prayer at the mosque is mandatory, and then the sense of incorporation is complete.

The fast of Ramadan and the annual pilgrimage, or *Hajj,* are both also deeply communal experiences. The fast holds the body social in a single ordinance curbing private instincts and grooming them into a shared obedience. The pilgrimage activates the centrality of Mecca within the consciousness of both actual participants and local communities everywhere vicariously engaged by the greeting of departees and their return and by the

concluding festival, *Al-Adha.* If we liken Muslim society
to a multiconcentric cluster of wheels around the
Meccan hub, then its spokes, from every corner of the
compass, point down to it in *Salat* and form the high-
ways or airways of the *Hajj.* That dual recruiting of geog-
raphy for a potent theology of direction is unique to
Islam as is also the massive physical centering of its people that pilgrimage achieves.

All these factors in the assurance of Islam—its inherent, ultimate, indubitable finality as the last of the faiths
given into history—are concluded, we might say, in the
Islamic state. Its role in the centuries of the Caliphate
simply perpetuated what Muhammad, *qua* ruler, had
attained. Muslims should always and only be Muslim-
ruled; and statehood, through all its vicissitudes and
vagaries, has been the pledge and means of true Islam.
There is no instinct of compunction about the reality
or the exercise of power. Divine omnipotence as
understood in Islam could hardly be congenially associated with what did not succeed or adequately fulfill
itself in the world as it is.

Herein, plainly, lies the supreme antithesis to
Christianity as inaugurated in the New Testament. It has
been wryly observed of Christianity in its realism about
the ultimate mystery of human evil, that the Christian
"does not suggest that all would be well with the world
if only God were a universal psycho-analyst" (Wells
1994:267). Muslim notions of *Dar al-Islam,* "the realm
of Islam," might suggest that all can be well if God were
in a universal Islamic polity, where all society is surren-
dered, all law is theocratic, and all power is Muslim.

A whole Islam is thus a formidable epitome of the
central themes of religion: beliefs, Scripture, structure,

ritual, community, and power so formidable as to be here aptly taken as a comprehensive test case of all that is at issue in secularity. If we can discern hope here, we will know its essentials anywhere. In what might it consist, and how might it be credited?

iii

Note has already been taken of Muslims in permanent minority situations and face-to-face with secular culture, lacking statehoods exclusively their own. The issues, therefore, are in no way academic or abstract. These Muslims are in unavoidable self-scrutiny. So indeed are many in securely Islamic polity yet confronted with alien cultural patterns—or immersed in them—and also required to reconsider their political assumptions, thanks to strident current argument about what constitutes Islamic statehood. This cannot be a clear blueprint, being itself in flux and question. Pakistan demanded Islamic statehood and has been at pains ever since to know what it means.

Further, there is the ever-growing awareness that a de facto pervasive human exclusion of Allah, from worship, from mind, and from concern, exists and grows, and that apparently no harm comes from the negligence. The Qur'an itself often uses the memorable phrase about the pagans—that they live, think, and operate "to the exclusion of God" (min duni-Llahi). This follows fourteen centuries of Islamic truth, of Din and Shari'ah. There are even Muslims who refer to today's compromising Muslims as the very Jahiliyyah who antedated Muhammad's revelation from God.[5] It is too easy to insist that Islam covers the whole of life and that nothing can be secular, that is, outside divine concern.

If secularity cannot be denied as a fact, it may not be
ignored as a problem. The Qur'an itself witnesses clearly to a human autonomy, for otherwise we could not be
summoned to Islam. Must it not be a question why
Allahu akbar needs to be said at all, requires to be
urgently asserted even with angry fists in the air? If it
were axiomatic, saying it would be superfluous. Total
secularity in terms described in Chapter 3 confronts
believers with the paradox of caring for the
negligible/indispensable, the disregarded/omnipotent.
Or, conversely, the sacred is not an opinion or a dogma,
but a trust and a task.

A careful exploration of Islam in this context yields
mutatis mutandis, features belonging to any and every
faith, vis-à-vis contemporary secularity. Finality cannot
ignore time or it absconds from itself. Change will
always be its tribunal. The terms in which Islam is
"final" now are for Muslims to decide. Their Scripture
will be their main arbiter. There is a modern principle of
"nonrepugnancy" to its teachings—a criterion looser
than arguable "conformity."[6] Surah 3.7 refers to "passages categorical and passages allegorical," without
identifying how the differentiation works. The Sunni
Schools of Law have understood the Qur'an to be capable of responsible interpretation by reference to its
"occasions" in *wahy,* and other considerations.

The principle that "the Qur'an means what Muslims
find it to mean" implies a degree of responsible possession, but it is by no means uninhibited. Who are the
"right" Muslims to exercise the role of exegesis? Here
there is deep debate. If the ability is confined to "ulama,"
to those expert in the minutiae of *tafsir, fiqh,* and *hadith,*
they will likely resist the sort of initiatives desired by

technicians, surgeons, academics, and others in the throes of modern issues, some of which have concerned us in Chapter 3. The right to *Ijtihad,* or "enterprise" as this activity is called, is thus itself a theme of contention. If it is closed (as a *Bab,* or door) except to the rightly qualified, it will induce a fixity of mind inimical to change.

Inasmuch as *Ijtihad* is necessary to the emergence of any *Ijma',* or "consensus," the question of the range of access to it becomes crucial. For, in Sunni Islam, consensus of the community is vital to any legitimization of change. *Ijma'* is potentially an organ of development, but for that reason it remains itself an issue.[7] In any event, its availability is far more in the spheres of law than of doctrine. Seeing that the latter is often the tight tether of the former, the necessary theological scrutinies of heritage are very far to seek. Much modern scholarship, at least in Arab Islam, has been diverted into uncontentious fields, precisely because the Quranic doctrinal ones were so prickly and crisis prone.[8]

Even so, the Qur'an and the *Shari'ah* have been significantly receptive to new interpretations in respect of translatability, monogamy, female rights, eschatology, and criteria of Islamicity. Opinion has reconciled itself, with some visionary exceptions, to the demise of the Caliphate and with it, in some measure, the absolute necessity of a rigorous type of Muslim statehood—not to say an open debate between Muslim and Muslim as to who is the "authentic" one. The debate may currently seem silenced by fanaticism or bigotry, but these must be seen as the reactionary measure of how far in crisis Muslims are. Clamor is a very partial index to reality.

If, as we have argued, an ability to distinguish intelligently between the two forms of secularity and to forgo the need to rely on statehood are vital present needs, there belongs in Islam a concept fitted to satisfy them. It is that of *abrogation,* which has been courageously invoked by significant, if still minor, schools of thought. Admittedly, they may have extended it beyond what is arguably its due range, yet its potential is great for a de-politicized Islam becoming again what it was in the first thirteen years of Muhammad's *Sirah,* when he was only a preacher and Islam was—in secular parlance—"just a *religion."*

The significance of *naskh,* or "abrogation," needs careful exposition both for Islam's sake today and because it is germane to all religious expression. Central to an understanding of the Qur'an, abrogation means that what is later in the revelation abrogates what was earlier, if they do not tally. The effect is to have what obtains to politics override what obtains to preaching—if one wants to see the issues that way.[9] Abrogation is undoubtedly present. How far may it extend? The logic now used by some proposes abrogation in reverse. Let what was earlier abrogate what is later. This has the effect of restoring the essentials of Islam to their pre-Hijrah quality.

The rationale, wisely stated, is: If desirable liberation is to happen in Islam, it must be for Islamic reasons, arguably taken from within. Islam is too deeply and res-olutely a theism to be susceptible to arguments for secu-larity from secular philosophies or Western pressures, nor is it desirable that it should be. The case can be right-ly and effectively made from within. Let the post-Hijrah shape of power be read as valid *then,* an *ad hoc* solution for the chronically feuding society of seventh-century Arabia, but manifestly totally unsuited to the twenty-first century. Realize in Muhammad's spiritual message the right contemporary form soundly abrogating what was there and then, but should not be here and now.

This would significantly de-politicize Islam, or at least allow it to be compatible with open citizenship in shared society. Did not Islam have its fundamental (foundational) shape in Muhammad's verbal mission? Does not the *Shahadah* confess him as *Rasul-Allah*, "the messenger'—not the generalissimo—'of Allah"? One difficulty this liberating use of *naskh* encounters, however, is the fact that the post-Hijrah politicization enters into the very fabric of the Qur'an, amounts to more than a third of its contents, and is inseparable from the regular *tajwid*, or "recitation," of the text. Opponents strongly deny that so much that is integral could be subject to *naskh*, intended only for minor and legal matters. Nevertheless, implicitly the Qur'an, though sacrosanct, is not unambiguous and has to be interpreted by internal reference, with no separate passage immune from the implications of another. That could be a very liberating principle, especially with such vital rulings as "There is no (i.e., should not be) compulsion in religion" (2.256). What might interfaith debate make of "To you your religion and to me mine" (109.6)? Is it conciliatory or defiant? In these ways there are divergencies of possible comprehension where one may abrogate another irrespective of chronology.

iv

Both the Qur'an and the *Shari'ah* are thus capable of genuine amenability to the mind of the community of Muslims, or to those with initiative and vision among them. Historically, the Shi'ah and their subsects and

Sufism in its many shapes and accents have demon-
strated that Islam, for all its formidable decisiveness, is
in no way monolithic. What matters is not the bare fea-
sibility, but the impetus and direction of creative "finality" responsive to contemporary demands. Among
these the favorable reckoning with secular political
power and the adequate surmounting of godless secularization are entirely within the range of Islamic
sources and of Muslim mentality.

Thus far our focus on Muslim dimensions has only
been to argue that these exemplify what the religious
mind has to address in responding anywhere to secularity—the ability to discern and appreciate the religious
validity of a ring-holding state-polity, not excluding but
not enthroning a single dominant historical tradition;
the readiness of majority and minority to cooperate
within such a setup; and the readiness of mind to
engage, by insight, compassion, and honesty, with the
confusions, pretensions, and tragedies belonging to outright secularity. These qualities may be far to seek.
Rigorism, whatever the religion involved, tends to polar-
ize all issues and to see only subversion in any challenge
to self-scrutiny. That is why it is right, in part, to speak
of "the secular experience of God," seeing that the claim
of God is coming through, even to the most aggressive of
God-sponsors, in the very reason to doubt themselves.

In the present climate, it would seem that fundamentalisms are in strong flow. For some Western
observers, Islam appears to be nothing else. That
impression is both premature and immature.[10]
Orthodoxy in Judaism has its own constraints. In both
cases reasons are partly political, and history has much
liability for them. With contemporary Christianity,

there are three distinctive factors to be explored that may well illuminate how the necessary sensitivities noted in the previous paragraph might be nurtured elsewhere among the faiths in response to both meanings of the secular. Exploring them, to conclude this chapter, will be a useful prelude to the next, which has to do with how Christians might intelligently relate to other faiths in their encounter with the secular.

The three factors are the Christian perception of Scripture, the original stance of the church in relation to political power, and—underlying both—the Christian fusion into one sovereignty of the divine and the crucified.

We have argued that because of their perception and reception of the Qur'an, Muslims could never be other than "fundamentalist," by virtue of verbatim, Arabic revelation. We have shown reason why this need not mean "fundamentalist" in the popular current sense.[11] With the Christian Scriptures on the other hand, no fundamentalism ever ought to arise, for they are not that sort of Scripture. To be sure, there are Christians who, so to speak, "Quranize," or make a Qur'an, out of the New Testament, despite the very nature of Gospels and epistles being against the idea. (The Gospels document a personality in a history; the epistles pastorally edify and unify a new community rawly out of paganism or Judaic exceptionality.)

This literature, so clearly sequential to a primary revelation in "the Word made flesh," is truly to be perceived as inspired and enabled for the task. "Holy men wrote as they were moved by the Holy Spirit." But they are plainly writing what is derivative *qua* text from what was/is primary *qua* personhood in Christic action.

Christians ought always to be clear what is, and can only be, the basic meaning to "the Word of God," namely, "God in Christ." As they do, they will rightly divide the word of truth that houses him. Rightly dividing it— that is, exegeting it—they will not mistake it for a heavenly deliverance bypassing the Incarnation and the Holy Spirit, but see it as the primary, fit to be canonized documenting of these realities. The Scriptures do not send the Holy Spirit into redundancy, but presuppose the Holy Spirit's ever-present ministry through the mind of a responsible, worshiping, living church.

The previous chapter sufficiently reviewed, within its limit, the readiness, indeed the necessity, of original Christianity to be innocent of state-power, to have its being solely as a divine society in grace and peace. Despite centuries of power-aegis and citizen-believer ideology, Christians today need find no essential problem, though maybe incidental ones, in conceding the secular state, the political order that—consistent with the viability and dignity of public good itself—allows all faiths indiscriminately, even if having long historic links with one especially. It will also be a Christian duty to encourage other faiths to perceive the same vocation, so that where dominance persists, it refrains from being oppressive and finds the logic for restraint in its own conscience.

That process may well be long and tedious. Privilege does not easily learn to forego itself. Vested interests of hierarchy persist. Tolerance can always be read as subversive, yet only if what obduracy protects demands to be subverted. Faiths have to come to perceive political secularity as both an appeal for and a call to truer religion, and thereby a more fitting worship of any God of truth. Oftentimes the recognition of the will of God comes in the relinquishment of a perceived willfulness of our own. There could be something very Islamic about that perception. For "letting God be God" at times requires the surrender of our own supposed management of divine ends and purposes.

The third Christian dimension is the one that long ago understood, and indeed dramatized, what total secularity, the human repudiation of transcendence, must mean in the experience of God. It belongs with the cross, an event that became a symbol, and thereby a faith-reading of the things the Godness of God means and undergoes. These wore a crown of thorns. These belonged with wood and nails. They had to do with a ministry that epitomized divine outspoken grace and truth yet culminated in a crucifixion that expressed "the sin of the world." In that nexus of suffering and glory, in both symbol and history, there was born a doxology—these are always at the heart of theology—that gathered a multitude of humankind, comprehending all races, around what could only be "the throne of God and of the Lamb." If these three elements of divine Christology are fitted to relate Christians readily to secular statchoods and to enable them patiently to disentangle and reverse the trends and foibles of secular agnosticism, the question must arise: Can they be mediated and commended to other faiths in their responses and anxieties in a secularized or secularizing world? If so, how?

5

Mission with the God of Patience

The expression "the God of patience" (Rom. 15:5) is surely among the most striking phrases of the New Testament. *Al-Sabur,* "the Patient," figures among the traditional names of God in Islam. What meaning can we give to this language? Paul's Greek word *hupomone* denotes "endurance under adversity," or "tenacity" and "staying power." How can these be descriptives of divine sovereignty? Can the meaning ever be "possessive" in respect of the divine? Or must it be only a quality of those who trust and depend on God as responsive to their reliance or worthy of it? There is a long perception of divine forbearance, even pathos, in the Judaic tradition.[1] How, in any theology, can this implication of divine nonimmunity in the human realm be reconciled with glory, dominion, power, and worship?

"Nonimmunity" is a negative cautiously phrased, perhaps fearing to say "vulnerable." But why fear? Any credible concepts of divine creation of the world and its entrustment to human dominion are plainly measures of an infinite self-limitation. They cannot be and not be. They spell risk. Other wills are now in play, unless all is vacuous—in which case the sovereignty also disappears. If we have understood our human experience aright, there is what the New Testament calls *kenosis* in the very being of God. To be divine is to be vicarious, to have undertaken partnership, to have enlisted for essential purposes what may nevertheless be withheld as a fact of the partnership. Nonimmunity has to be turned into a positive and understood as deliberate participation.

Need it then surprise us if modern secularity constitutes a present dimension of what has always been divinely risked, namely, a partnership unwanted and a human destiny misread? May it not be proper, then, to think and speak of "the secular experience of God" meaning this negligibility, this disregard, this rearing of altars in vulgarity "from those whom it does not concern"?

The factors prompting it are evident enough: weariness with the miscarriages of truth in religious dogma and of spiritual mystery in their rituals; the fascination of technologies that seem to argue the entire enthronement of the human factor and the utter exclusion of God; and the burden of how "stale and unprofitable seem all the uses [and abuses] of this world." In face of all these, the patience of God will seem a strange mockery or a sad delusion—unless, perhaps, they are the very realms in which we should detect it. For what is technology if not a gift bestowed with the patient time in which to reach its current apex? For, however precarious and menacing, as well as impressive, nuclear fission and the information revolution are, they are no more, in principle, than the shaping of a spade or the driving of a plow. And what are miscarriages of truth if not divine risks, the evidence of a transcendence in perpetual patience?

We do not seem to be tracing, in all these, the *impa*tience of God. Not here any divine "wearying of mankind" in withdrawal of the mystery of being. As for the sundry evidences of human "wearying of the world," is not its deepest burden the sense of an absence? And may not the sense of an absence be a question of the right clues about a presence? Job's anguish is not about *whether* but rather about *where* he might find the redeemer he knew there must be. There could be no point to his sort of anxiety in a world so deprived of God as to admit no quest for him. All must turn on where the quest leads and on what it proves to find.

It is here that Christian faith finds itself realized in "the God with wounds," as it was once finely said, "the Almighty who has shed human tears."[3] The *Deus patiens* of the Gospels is known as such in Christ crucified, where history holds the enactment of what belonged in eternity "before the foundation of the world." Relating directly to what embodied "the sin of the world," the human wrongness self-defined, the Cross stands as both event and symbol, as both the act and the cost of redemptive love, disclosing the divine nature. "God in Christ" must mean "the Christ in God," the expression in time of the grace by which we may interpret and understand all else. "God with us" in these terms is our frame of reference "in knowledge and love of God." Their way with us has always been the way of patience. This understanding of divine grace, bearing our sins and suffering to reconcile is seen to be the deepest relevance of what we have been calling "the secular experience of

God." The Cross of Christ proved the farthest reach of what our autonomy and freedom might mean to the God who "suffered" them to be—and to be as the Cross would prove them.[4] This, then, is "the Gospel of God" that most fully answers both the searching wistfulness and the chronic willfulness of secularity as explored in Chapter 3.

ii

If, then, "the God of patience" be so, how may Christian faith fulfill the trust of it vis-à-vis the incidence, for other faiths, of the two kinds of contemporary secularity?

That the Christian sense of mission is in crisis is not in doubt. The increasing sense of the irreducible "thereness" of plural religions in the life and story of the world gives pause to the old ambition to Christianize the whole. That may have seemed feasible at the opening of this twentieth century, when European powers—Britain, France, the Netherlands, and Belgium—held political sway over most of humankind, and when Islam, at the demise in 1924 of its long Caliphate, could be seen as in disruption."[5] The staying power of Hinduism, Buddhism, and Islam—however storm-tossed in modernity—is now more evident.

It was possible for leading missionary figures in Christian counsels to call for "the evangelization of the world in this generation," as John R. Mott put it. At best, that could only be had in sheer geographical terms, planting personnel in lands as yet without them. But mission has always been more than geographical. "Go ye into all the world" means more than a travel agency. It means a going into the heart of cultures and the depths of creeds and codes as well as into the width of the world. Ships and stations and compounds were the means of mission often only sadly proximate to its ends.

The early Christians were certainly educated in their task by the very fact of their going. They learned to baptize new vocabulary as well as personal recruits and to find organs for their purpose that came into necessity only because they were translating into a wider scene. The very shape of the New Testament as literature indicates a learning as well as a teaching church. Perhaps it may be the same today. Mission and theology have always been defining each other. What are the lessons now? Has there been or need there be a loss of nerve?

The questions press because of the many factors tending to the emergence of "dialogue"—that overworked theme. How does it relate to mission? The latter implies personal conversion, the recruitment and baptism of the individual who responds. The former seems to mean: "Let us courteously compare notes, cooperate where we can, and remain peacefully what we are." The idea has much to commend it, for it serves to abate bigotry, to curb the pride of the "only us" mentality, and to facilitate common action in urgent matters of public good and communal harmony.

Yet "dialogue" seems to reduce conviction to academic status. Does Islam exist to be discussed, or Christ to be compared? Are not faiths necessarily to be obeyed, seeking not discourse, but discipleship? Proselytism, the eliciting of adherents, is often now the deplorable thing that dialogue would banish. Yet in original Greek, *proselytos* was simply one who was asking, even yearning, to understand and deserving to be told. Is there no place for him or her now? If mission may no longer anticipate and receive discipleship, what remains of it?

Certainly this self-interrogation, at least within Christian circles, has sharpened in recent decades. Many Christians are more ready to sustain Christian Aid, compassion for its own sake, than evangelism with or without it. Uncertainty about faith-proclamation entails perplexity around truth-issues. For some the old assurance seems suspect; for others, in reaction, it demands to be more absolutely asserted and obeyed.

What always needs to be said is that Christian faith is inherently hospitable. Its charter is "Whoever so wills may come." It can never be a closed shop, accessible only to those rightly born, culturally acceptable, or otherwise desirable. It sings of a kingdom opened to all believers, and the sole criterion of believing is faith. The church can never be maneuvered, in fact or by implication, into accepting to be a community only for those bearing its name. It is never hereditary, but personal. It intends to "make" disciples, but not only in individual terms. Thus mission and sincerity interdefine themselves. The church would never have existed if it had not been composed of those who once did not belong. It betrays its own being if it ceases to be in missionary hope and will and energy.

That basic conviction, however, returns us to the problems. If the issue is not *whether* about mission, then *how*? The case made here holds the person always in its sight, but requires that Christianity think also of mission to other faiths in themselves, as there in the world scene, as nations sharing in United Nations organization, as carrying enormous liabilities for the peace, sanity, health, and hope of vast populations of humanity. This sense of things can also vitally affect a ministry of truth vis-à-vis the individual, in terms of liberty of thought, freedom of association, and the right to self-responsibility. For response to perceived truth by way of soul-conversion has long been impeded or fraught with unacceptable loneliness and peril. Those who look to convert had better also look to what converting entails—burdens in the psyche, the family, and the society—that make it scarcely viable.

However, aside from what it might mean in respect of freedom to think and believe and act on the appeal of faith, ministry to other religions has its own proper warrant. It does not mean patronage, religious imperialism, or any trace of condescension. It frankly recognizes the givenness of other faith systems, however it may resolve, or fail to resolve, the providence in the fact. It realizes that the several faiths are differently confronted by the same issues from a ubiquitous secularity, and that Christian perceptions may well be mediated and interpreted precisely in that common milieu and be the more relevant for being common to them all.

iii

This brings us back to dialogue and its relevance for unforfeited mission. This dialogue, initially, strives to make the vital distinction, earlier explored, between secularity understood as the neutrality of state-power about the religious allegiance of all subjects, and secularity as a total indifference to, or rejection of, transcendent meaning and duty. The reasons for, and the urgency of, that distinction will need to be painstakingly argued as far as possible from *within* the criteria by which other faiths are guided.

This will mean their arriving at a quality of humility that is genuinely prepared to serve, rather than dictate, the mind of society. It will have to argue that in the final analysis faith is truest when out of privilege and into liberty. On the one hand, believing will be a private question *qua* law and status as citizen; but on the other hand, this will not render it a private option so that its content consists only in one's having chosen it. The distinction may be difficult for those inured to state-aegis or divine-imposition, but duly realizing it will not alter the *spiritual* sanction its contents have.

Is it not precisely here that conviction becomes more rightly mine when it has been free to know itself as thoroughly faithful in *not* being sanctioned otherwise? To be sure, many sanctions of culture, rearing, tradition, and the religious community will legitimately remain, but they will be the more fully religious in that alternative communities have the same sanctions in their own idiom and are now liberated from any legal inferiorization. When minorities are free, majorities will be healthier too. There will also be the stimulus of the hope that, under the United Nations Charter of Human Rights, religious freedom has the merit of being multilateral.

All this may be far to seek in Muslim and some Buddhist lands—a consideration that only makes advocacy of it the more urgent. Though Christian faith is well contrived to present the idea, it has to be cherished from within each faith as continuous with all that the acknowledgment of a de facto pluralism has to mean. Traditionally, Islam has divided the world into *Dar al-Islam* and *Dar al-Harb,* the realm-Islamic and the realm of necessary *Jihad* to make it so. Around the fourteenth and fifteenth centuries it was realized, only for political, tactical reasons, that either party, Muslim and Christian, had to coexist. So the concept of *Dar al-Sulh* reluctantly emerged—"a realm of armistice" in which trade might be mutually pursued, maybe "Capitulations"[6] granted and advantages accrued to both parties.

Something like those Capitulations has now to be ventured, by which faiths could look out and identify what they can accede[7] to with each other—the doctrines and aspirations they genuinely have in common, if they would but realize. This is part of the role of dialogue, so that these may be identified and, to a degree, possessed as common. This does not mean compromise of what must and will remain at odds; it only makes it more conversable by virtue of contrasted interrelevance.[8] In this way, it may be hoped that wise mission can fulfill itself, while communal well-being will be making good the obligations of any statehood rightly alerted to the trust it carries.

Writing of inner Christian divisions about the nature of the Christian Sacrament, the old Puritan writer Thomas Fuller warned: "It is to be feared lest our long quarrels about the manner of His presence cause the matter of His absence, for our want of charity to receive Him." May not the stresses of learning to be ecumenical within Christendom have some bearing on the interrelation of religions? It might be thought that, in some respects, the asperities are no greater even though the affinities be less. Either way, part of Christian vocation is to be ready to look for what reconciles in the significance of what divides and so to elucidate the latter as to serve the former.

iv

What of outright secularity, as pondered in Chapter 3? Should we fear that the depoliticizing of religion in state-neutrality plays into its hands? Hardly—or only if the final and proper ground of faith is state protection. We need to see that sacred and secular interpenetrate. On any doctrine of creation and human dignity, there are autonomies. The secular sphere is potential of sacredness, but we humans have to do the hallowing. Correspondingly, the sacred is a vocation that waits upon our doing. This means that the sacred proceeds improperly if it relies altogether on law and enforcement. If we claim to organize, systematize, and legalize the sacred—as in the time of medieval papacy or in the prevailing instincts of Islam—we go far to secularize the sacred itself. The two realms cannot be absorbed together simply by asserting, as Muslims do, that they are not distinguishable. Indeed they are not separable: But the nature of their indivisibility is such that the secular is there to be hallowed, while the sacred seeks out what the secular must become. Law and order, a familiar pair, have some part in this, mainly in restraining: the full constraining in freedom comes only by truth and love. The "being," in either case, cannot be other than a "becoming."

These are perhaps abstractions, but necessary even so. Mission with the God of patience in a secularity thoroughly refusing, despising, or deploring its sacred meanings will be guided by the clue we have studied concerning what that patience is as measured in the Cross. The aim of such a mission will be to kindle into life this perception in order to interrogate its neglect. It will want to have other faiths realize the limitations of what law can do. It will deepen any sense of disquiet, or absence of meaning, or unease that secularity generates in many. It will also need to be honest about the factors in religion that have alienated sensitive souls. It will, therefore, be set to invite believers, of any system, away from hardness of heart and toward a sense of their own doubtfulness. Religions are expert at supposing themselves intrinsically credible and vindicated in their own eyes.[9] There are some forms of possession of Christ's gospel that "de-commend" it by the very shape of their witness. An impatience of God has no place in the gospel of the Cross.

If Christian relationships, thus inwardly circum-spect, can help move other faiths toward some reverent doubt of themselves, such mission may well serve them better to possess their truths. There is everything right about the ambition of Islam to have God "all in all," to be zealous for *Allahu akbar;* or the desire of the Buddhist to have every "secular self" know that there is a crisis in "your being you." Yet in either case, the God of patience wills to be Lord by grace alone and wants the self to know the crisis for what it is around the true des-tiny, not the renunciation, of desire.

Which ear—including our own pair—is deaf? Some secularity hears only the voice of the laboratory, the tech-nique, the cry of "Let us, seeing we can," and so is deaf to other realms of reference. Some secularity hears only the cry of the market and the greed of gain. These are aspects of what Amos of old called a "famine of hearing the words of the Lord" (Amos 8:11). But whereas famines usually engender a hunger for relief, these have first to be made aware of themselves—a paradox that takes us far into the nature of the secularity that has lost its own clues.

Or, in every case, has it? Any mission with the God of patience has to be sensitive to wistfulness. Some sec-ularity, to be sure, is brash, vulgar, or self-willed; but more is anxious and puzzled. If we believe we are entrusted with the grace of God in Christ, there must be grace in the trust. One clear aspect of this must be the inner strains and tensions in other faith communities through the pressures of change and the bewilderments of the situation. For example, pressures arise in the generation gap where the older is at odds with the younger. Will it be "patient" here to think only in terms of winning allegiance, or might that be a form of self-seeking that needs to be curbed by care for human needs? Relation to how secular environments impinge on minority loyalties can be had only through the resources of each faith's own heritage. These may be helped and sifted by a wise Christian relationship alerted to their frames of reference. It may well be in this context of a deeper internal awareness and scrutiny of themselves, that discovery within other faiths of the relevance of Christ may duly come. Aggressive relations bent only or primarily on recruitment may have failed the God of patience in the name of a God of zeal. The gentler way may be the more loyal.

A deep Christian commitment to mission may be asking here whether the whole argument has forgotten how far religions—all of them—may be demonic in their pride, their spiritual tyranny, their sense of righteous merit. Do not people need to be saved? Does not the idea of Christian mission to faiths as such really leave out the whole revolutionary goal of its program? Are we supposing that divine grace has less to do than we hitherto thought?

Those issues are urgent, but are we to go back on being ready to concede de facto pluralism and ignore the practical and theological obligations it lays on us?

Inviting people to "salvation" needs to undertake all the
leading questions about how they understand the term,
if religious, and, if secular, what it can possibly mean.
These will inevitably lead us back into what, at its
soundest, dialogue had come to see. We are serving the
God of patience not, to be sure, the God of confusion,
but also not, the God of other than the human world.[10]
Insofar as people are deceptive and perverse, there will
always be a necessity for them to be "saved" from their
systems, but also, in that these are culture and life,
saved in and with them. Nor is the meaning of "saving"
confined to the mystery of eternal destiny.

That the meaning and yearning of Christian mission
center on personal coming into "the knowledge and love
of God" as that knowledge and love are ours in Christ, is
not and may not be in doubt. It coexists with a legitimate vocation to the perennial inner awareness of other
faiths as they inform and constrain their societies. It
coexists also with the perspectives, idle or serious, bland
or significant, of the wholly secular-minded.

The superficial among the latter surely concern the
God of patience in the ways Jesus had us understand in
the story of the younger son in the familiar parable.[11]
The logic of the far country has to register its slow and
often sordid findings, while the father waits, unchanged,
nonvindictive, compassionate, and wistful. Only on the
implicit, unexamined assumption that this is so can the
son at length resolve: "I will arise and go to my father."
He takes it for granted, and rightly, that his father is still
his, on those forgiving terms, though he does not know
the cost of it in the father's heart. It is just this "ring and
robe," this "singing and dancing" in the father's house
that tell the nature of God whenever the secular world

comes to itself and comes home. Mission can live only to serve that confidence. Shakespeare discerned it well when he wrote in sonnet 129:

> Mad in pursuit and in possession so,
> Had, having, and in quest to have, extreme;...
>> All this the world well knows; yet none knows well
>> To shun the heaven that leads men to this hell.

"Well," that is, in how far "the far country" lies. What we know not how "to shun," we can in Christ forsake.

As for the secularity that is in no way perverse but high-minded, the Christian has at once to recognize an ally and to resolve a puzzle. It is notable that many who hold strongly to duty, integrity, reverence, and a sense of transcendent liability began so from a Christian nurture they came later to relinquish or to despise.[12] The reasons must be the Christian's concern, but the implications are clear. It is as if these minds might be, as it were, in "the left hand of God." The right hand has long been a biblical symbol of divine sovereignty, the sovereignty with the Christ credentials. The task of the church will be to enable other faiths to receive them though not owning the Christ-symbol for themselves. That duty will still leave on Christ's people the onus of commending the credentials where their idealism is finally secured, namely, in word and sacrament, in the Christ-insignia of things divine.

There is one final present aspect of things that seems to confirm this conclusion about Christian faiths in the midst of the religions and the ideologies of good. It is that old-style evangelism by "sent" agents is no longer feasible in many countries. Visas are denied or laws prohibit. Often what presently thinks of itself as mission is resolved into chaplaincies, finds its *raison d'être* in ensuring worship and pastoral ministry in expatriate communities with trading, technical, educational, and other functions. It is these people who commend faith by coexisting in work, residence, and shared community. Conversely, missionaries have become "fraternal workers" or "sisters in ministry," where churches are self-governed by national minorities in full control in their own milieu.

These facts would seem to tally with the theme we have explored where mission *to* becomes mission *in*. Maybe what is true practically is also what has to be true theologically. Could it be that the long, arduous, and patient experience of mission leads us back to where it all began in the meaning of incarnation—the Incarnation of God?

Notes

Chapter 1: Exploring an Irony

1. It is the instinct for "worldwide-ness" that made the New Testament the sort of document it is, with "epistles" not to "races" as such, but to "places." The Gospels, too, come into being because communities, dispersed far from where it all began, need to learn their historical origins in place and time.

2. See E. R. Dodds (1965) for discussion of paganism as essentially rituals performed rather than "beliefs" affirmed. For practical reasons, atheism was not an option, nor disavowal of the sovereignty of Caesar.

3. "Left to roam as he will" is another translation. Bits in camels' mouths were familiar enough to Muhammad's nomad hearers. There may well be allusions also to the certainty of final judgment, as in the immediate context in Surah 75.

4. This verse has been too long cited in total miscomprehension as if it were about a pious quietism. The Greek *entos* means "among your ranks," "in your actual midst." "You," of course, is plural, not the private introverted self, but the active fellowship with tasks in the world because "the kingdom" is divine energy indwelling discipleship in its truth.

Chapter 2: The Realm of Politics and Law

1. This witticism plays on Descartes' familiar *Cogito ergo sum*, "I think and so I am," which shaped modern philosophy

in its focus on "knowing" via empiricism, as the crux about any metaphysics.

2. *Ab initio* with the proviso that Islam begins in the thirteen years through which Muhammad was only a messenger. Islam, however, dates its calendar, not from that initiation but from the emigration that inaugurated statehood and power.

3. The clear distinction here between accession to Muhammad's rulership or regime and actual faith in his message is emphatic. After his death some adherents reverted from Islam believing that their loyalty was to the man only, a loyalty that lapsed on his demise. They had to be disillusioned by Abu Bakr.

4. This is what happened after Meccan Quraish capitulated to Muhammad. Why should pagans still acknowledge deities who had failed in contest with the Allah of this prophet? Education into faith can always follow formal surrender.

5. "Imperial" here by long hindsight in that a vast Caliphate came into being from Sind to Spain. There is evidence, however, that initially what were no more than raids grew into conquest by sheer momentum of success.

6. See, for example, Arnold (1896), written to accentuate "preaching" to rebut the concept of an "Islam spread by the sword." It seems clear, though, that the first Muslims were sometimes reluctant to spread their faith to all and sundry lest this might dilute their cherished Arabic identity.

7. For example, Maulana Abu-l-Kalam Azad, who strongly pleaded for all-India unity. See Douglas (1988).

8. Political Zionism, prior to the Second World War, had much to do to overcome powerful Jewish rejection of, or reluctance for, its logic of necessary statehood. It was the near miracle of 1967 that rallied the ideology of diaspora Judaism to the Zionist cause.

9. A notable example is the *Journal of the Institute of Muslim Minority Affairs.* Based in London, it is tackling resourcefully the many issues confronting Islam in the European context.

10. It could not credibly be "Judea" or "the Jewish State." There were other considerations also. The Constitution chose to phrase its theological reference: "the Rock of Israel," because of tensions between Orthodox and irreligious Jews.

11. These are the words used in the British Coronation Liturgy, said to the Sovereign when the Orb is presented—the symbol of authority, but only under God-in-Christ.

12. Hooker's seminal work has its meaning in its very title. Burke saw spiritual "establishment" as indispensable to the safe and sane society government existed to ensure. The Oxford Tractarians, Keble and Newman, had the same idea in detecting "national apostacy" in a reformed Parliament bringing greater honesty into the system of bishoprics in Ireland and thereby infringing "sacred institutions" and abandoning the due role of an "Anglican" state.

13. This odd phrase was used in the Balfour Declaration of November 1917, which never mentioned Palestinians by name, though it referred to "Palestine." The Declaration paved the way for a Palestinian Mandate of the League of Nations in 1919/20 committed—in some sense—to "a national home for the Jewish people" in Palestine. This ideological negligibility of Palestinians has been a feature ever since.

14. It is noteworthy how Zionists drew examples from Italian unification and nationality consciousness in Europe: e.g., Hess (1945), Pinsker (1944), Herzl (1955:221–313), and the speeches of Max Nordau. In aiming to galvanize the ghetto mind, they even used some of the jibes of the anti-Semites themselves.

15. See, for Muslim example, An-Na'im (1990).

Chapter 3: The Theme in Sex and Culture

1.   It is significant that the usage is now developing of "*loving* relationships," as if the adjective could only obtain in homosexual terms. This is monstrously unreal.

Chapter 4: The Shape of the Religious Mind

1. One can speak of "basic," or "integral"; "very important" or "essential." But *asasi, asli, hamm jiddan, jawhari* all fail to carry the desired meaning. To fall back on "fanatical" or "obscurantist" would not quite convey.

2. Using the word without the capital "M" denotes a submission to God antedating, or not conforming to, the "capitalizing" of *islam* that came only via Muhammad and the Pillars of Religion.

3. Muslims often regard Christianity as too ideal in its ethic of nonresistance, or its theology of marriage as unsuited to the actualities of human nature. Judaism, although having a valid prophetic strain, went astray into ethnicizing divine election and grace. Islam, by contrast, is practicable and universal.

4. The term repeatedly employed as limiting Muhammad's role is *al-balagh,* "the communication," the verbal mission.

5. This term denoted the "ignorance" and "wildness" preceding Islam. Notable in describing de facto Egyptian Islam this century as in *Jahiliyyah* were Sayyid Qutb and Muhammad al-Ghazali.

6. The term was often used in and concerning the Basic Principles Committee during constitution-making debates in Pakistan, with a reference committee of "*ulama*" to take stock of it.

7. Shi'ah Islam differs in these areas in vital respects. Space forbids any discussion of them here.

8. Cases in point are Taha Husain in *'Ala Hamish al-Sirah* (1933), a study "in the margins of prophethood and tradition," and Fazlur Rahman (1980)—a scholar virtually ousted from Pakistan for his venturesome ideas.

9. The proviso is important if, as often, *naskh* is held to concern only moot, or minor, points of law.

10. Reasons why, and clear evidences to the contrary, are studied in Cragg (1994).

11. See actual or potential debate against "fundamental-ism" in, e.g., Khwaja (1977) and, partially, Akhtar (1990 and 1987).

Chapter 5: Mission with the God of Patience

1. Note, especially, the many writings of Rabbi Abraham Heschel. See discussion and bibliography in Cragg (1992b: chap. 6).

2. The meaning here is not the secularity in Chapter 2, but only that in Chapter 3.

3. Disraeli, the Victorian Tory Prime Minister of Britain, has a character in his novel *Tancred* (1890:168) use these words.

4. "Suffered" here has an apt double sense—the older English "allowed to be" (as in "Suffer the children to come...") and the more usual "undergo at the hands of..."

5. Cf. the report of the Jerusalem meeting of the International Missionary Council in the spring of 1928.

6. The Ottomans granted these concessions to consuls and foreign communities to cover trading and extraterritorial consular jurisdictions. It took them some time to realize that they could solicit concessions in reverse in Europe.

7. "Accede" is a happier word than "concede," because "concede" implies reluctance or chagrin. Interfaith mutuality of content, however minimal, has to be eager and gentle.

8. Some attempt was made in Cragg (1986).

9. See, for example, discussion of the place of penitence about themselves on the part of religions in Cragg (1992a).

10. The phrase is proper, though we must reserve the possibility expressed by the poet Alice Meynell: "God may have other words for other worlds."

11. See this study in Bailey (1973).

12. Many nineteenth-century writers exemplify this fact, e.g., George Eliot and Matthew Arnold. There are many, like Thomas Hardy, who stay wistfully where they no longer remain intellectually. It is a situation very relevant to the patience of God.

References Cited

Akhtar, Shabbir. 1990. *A Faith for All Seasons*. London: Bellew Publishing Co.

———. 1987. *Reason and the Radical Crisis of Faith*. New York: Peter Lang.

al-Faruqi, Isma'il. 1982. *Islamization of Knowledge: General Principles and Work-Plan*. Washington: International Institute of Islamic Thought.

An-Na'im, Abdullahi Ahmed. 1990. *Toward an Islamic Reformation: Civil Liberties, Human Rights, and International Law*. Syracuse: Syracuse University Press.

Arnold, Thomas. 1896. *The Preaching of Islam*. London: A. Constable & Co.

Bailey, Kenneth. 1973. *The Cross and the Prodigal*. St. Louis: Concordia Publishing House.

Cragg, Kenneth. 1986. *The Christ and the Faiths*. Philadelphia: Westminster Press.

———. 1992a. *To Meet and to Greet*. London: Epworth Press.

———. 1992b. *Troubled by Truth*. Edinburgh: Pentland Press.

———. 1994. *Returning to Mount Hira*. London: Bellew Publishing Co.

Disraeli, Benjamin F. 1890. *Tancred*. London: Longmans, Green & Co.

Dodds, E. R. 1965. *Pagans and Christians in an Age of Anxiety*. Cambridge: Cambridge University Press.

Douglas, Ian H. 1988. *Abu-l-Kalam Azad: An Intellectual and Religious Biography*. Ed. by Gail Minault and Christian W. Troll. Delhi: Oxford University Press.

Hazlitt, William. 1906. *Characters of Shakespeare's Plays*. London: Dent.

Herzl, Theodor. 1896. *Der Judenstaat*. Vienna: n.p.

———. 1955. *Portrait for This Age*. Ed. with intro. by Ludwig Lewisohn. Pref. by David Ben-Gurion. New York: World Publishing Co.

Hess, Moses. 1945. *Rome and Jerusalem*. 2d ed. Trans. Meyer Waxman. New York: Bloch Publishing Co. German orig. 1862.

Hinchliff, Peter. 1982. *Holiness and Politics*. London: Darton, Longman, & Todd.

Husain, Taha. 1933. *'Ala Hamish al-Sirah*. Cairo: Dar al-Matba'ah. 3 vols.

International Missionary Council. 1928. *The Christian Life and Message in Relation to Non-Christian Systems of Thought and Life*. Vol. 1. London: International Missionary Council.

Khwaja, Jamal. 1977. *Quest for Islam*. Bombay: Allied Publishers, Ltd.

Murdoch, Iris. 1970. *The Sovereignty of Good*. London: Routledge & Kegan Paul.

Pinsker, Lev. S. 1944. *Road to Freedom: Writings and Addresses*. Intro. by B. Netanyahu. New York: Scopus. Includes essay: "Auto-emancipation: A Call to His People by a Russian Jew."

Potter, Dennis. 1984. *Waiting for the Boat: On Television*. London: Faber & Faber.

Rahman, Fazlur. 1980. *Major Themes of the Qur'an*. Minneapolis: Bibliotheca Islamica.

Sardar, Ziauddin. 1985. *Islamic Futures: The Shape of Ideas to Come*. New York: Mansell.

Shattuck, Roger. 1974. *Marcel Proust*. New York: Viking Press.

Warren, Max. 1955. *Caesar, the Beloved Enemy.* Naperville, Ill.: A. R. Allenson.

Wells, Stanley. 1986. *Complete Works of William Shakespeare.* Oxford edition. Vol. 3. London: S. Wells & G. Taylor.

———. 1994. *Shakespeare: A Dramatic Life.* London: Oxford University Press.

West, Nathanael. 1993. *Miss Lonelyhearts.* New York: New Directions.

Wilder, Thornton. 1927. *The Bridge of San Luis Rey.* New York: Grosset & Dunlap.

Woolf, Virginia. 1980. *Diaries.* Vol. 3. Ed. A. O. Bell. New York: Harcourt, Brace, Jovanovich.